NEARLY A HERO

To

Syd & Dorothy

with best wishes

David Windsor

David Windsor

NEARLY A HERO

DJD Publications

Published in Great Britain in 1994
by D J D Publications

© D J Dicks (1994)

British Library Cataloguing in Publication Data

ISBN 0-9523812-0-6

Laserset in Palatino by
Ann Buchan (Typesetters), Middlesex

Printed and bound in Southampton by
Itchen Printers Limited

Foreword

Encouraged by the theory that everyone has at least one book inside them waiting to be hatched, I have at last put pen to paper.

The story written entirely from memory of events which happened fifty or more years ago is based on true facts with occasional slight deviations in the interests of discretion, decency or even poetic licence.

Most of the names have been changed, so if anyone thinks they recognise themselves I can only say 'If the cap fits. . .'

If some of the events and remarks seem to have racist overtones they are not intended to give offence, but merely to 'tell it as it was' fifty years ago.

Indeed the Race Relations Board may feel that thanks to their unceasing vigilance, congratulations are in order and that in many cases the wheel has turned full circle.

D.W.

To my father who was man enough to admit the bombs frightened him, yet brave enough to ignore the blitz and travel to the centre of London each night to help produce the Daily Herald

This book is dedicated to all Naval Telegraphist Special Operators. They came from all walks of life - from Bank Managers to bricklayers - but when duty called the Navy decided they were bright enough to be placed in a special corner.

It is especially dedicated to the men of HMS Aberdeen whose special corner turned out to be a mangrove swamp in West Africa where they rotted and fed the mosquitos for most of the war.

The Lion Awakes

My story begins at a Boys' Brigade Camp just outside
Paignton in Devon and it is August 1939. I was one of
some fifty or so teenagers, most of whom were destined
to become cannon-fodder, but at that moment were still
enjoying Neville Chamberlain's 'peace in our time'.

The sun was blazing down and had already taken its
toll. My particular chum affectionately known as 'Cockles' (later to become Sergeant Pilot Copple) was totter-
ing around on badly burnt legs wrapped up in tea-
leaves, while those of us still unaffected played cricket
or soccer and wrestled and squabbled with the enthusiasm of youth.

I came home on August 26th when the camp still had
a week to run. The remainder came home in a bit of a
hurry on September 3rd.

On that morning those of us already at home at-
tended bible class, for in spite of our tough activities of
regular physical training, football and boxing every
week, we were in the main a clean living bunch of lads
who respected women, rarely swore and were practising Christians.

With Neville Chamberlain's speech to the nation that Sunday morning that lifestyle would soon disappear for ever.

My main concern on hearing we were at war with Germany was that I was only sixteen and that I would surely miss all the action for the war was bound to be over by Christmas.

Little did I know. . .

Early Warning

After bible class I wandered over to Edmonton Recreation Ground with my friends to watch the football as usual and halfway through the second half, with the war scarcely an hour old, the sirens began wailing.

This was a crisis! The score was 2–2, the weather was fine — what did the rule book say?

There was a hasty conference in the centre circle and the skippers decided to play for a winning goal, which they did (if my memory serves me right, Winchester Rovers got the decider) and then we all ran home like the wind with irate Air Raid Wardens waving us off the streets.

I arrived at our Anderson Shelter slightly out of breath (it was the best part of two miles from the Rec) to find my mother and sister wiping tears of laughter from their eyes and my father clutching a dressing gown round himself.

Apparently he was in the bath when the sirens sounded and he arrived in the shelter dripping wet with only his longjohns on and dropped in at sixty m.p.h. on the rest of the family.

We Stood Alone

It was this capacity to laugh when things looked black that made Britain such a tough nut that Hitler couldn't crack, even when we stood alone against him for a whole year.

Eventually of course he postponed his plans to invade us and because he so desperately needed a result, he attacked Russia instead and with hindsight, that wasn't such a good idea either.

But I digress, we were now at war and in spite of our bitter experience twenty-five years previously, there was a tremendous enthusiasm throughout the country to show this fellow Hitler that this time he had gone too far. We had no idea how tremendously prepared he was and how tremendously unprepared we were and my generation had no idea of the horrors of the Somme and Passchendaele and the gross incompetence of our top brass in World War One.

Our history lessons had been about 1066, the Spanish Armada and the Gunpowder Plot — the truth about the Great War was too recent and unpalatable for school-children in the twenties and thirties. So jingoism prevailed and we set to with a will to do our bit.

The Edmonton Air Disaster

My father was no coward but he always expected the worse and provided against it. In 1938 I had been playing football in our street in Edmonton when one of my friends called out, 'look at that plane!' We stared up at a silver biplane which proved to be an RAF Gloucester Gladiator which was plunging earthwards. It crashed on some houses near Pymmes Park and black smoke billowed into the sky.

We ran to the spot but by the time we arrived the police had already cordoned off the area and the rescue services were hard at work. It was an appalling disaster, many people were killed, some heroically trying to free the pilot as the plane exploded, and I had never seen devastation like it.

When I returned home and poured my story out to the family, my father summed up the situation with the words 'If there is another war, that disaster will be like a drop in the ocean'. I thought of that horrific scene I'd just left and was sure he was exaggerating.

Once again, little did I know. . .

Now on the first day of the war my father again summed up the situation. Obviously we've got to come into London to work, but I'll rent a place in the country for a few weeks to see how it goes.

The Phoney War

Within two days we had a house in St Albans and I found myself cycling back to Edmonton every morning where I was employed at the local print shop as an apprentice compositor in my third year, at the princely sum of eighteen shillings a week, which was fifty per cent more than I started at in 1937. My father was a proof reader on the Daily Herald and consequently commuted right to the centre of the city and to his eternal credit, in spite of his cautious manner, he went there by any means at his disposal (like most working class men he had no car) right through the Blitz and everything else Hitler could throw at London for five devastating years.

The Royal Oak

However, the early months of the war were proving an anti-climax. Barely a shot was being fired other than at sea where the U-boats were beginning to flex their muscles and, indeed, rocked the Royal Navy back on their heels with a devastating blow when Lieutenant Prien, Commander of the U47, entered Holm Sound and by squeezing past the blockships, found a gap in the hitherto impregnable naval base at Scapa Flow and sunk the Royal Oak with the loss of some eight hundred hands. This to me was the most brilliant and audacious naval attack of the whole war and was of the stuff my heroes were made of. Too bad he had to be a Kraut!

However, Scapa was a long way away and England was exceedingly tranquil, so my father decided to move the family back to Edmonton, for which I was truly thankful.

The Scarf

Through the winter nights my sister knitted an enormous khaki scarf (I began to wonder if she knew how to stop it, for like Topsy it grew and grew) for her boyfriend who was residing peacefully in France with the BEF, and at weekends I used to cycle to Kings Langley (some twenty three miles each way) to see my first girlfriend, whose father had also left our street on hearing Mr Chamberlain's words and transferred from teaching at Edmonton County to Hemel Hempstead.

Like most teenage affairs it didn't last but for six months it kept me in good condition cycling there and back.

In Spring 1940 we had a glimpse of things to come when the Germans invaded Denmark and Norway, and

I remember how I glowed with enthusiasm when we promptly sent an Expeditionary Force to Norway to throw the Germans out.

First Round to Hitler

By the end of April it was obvious we had bitten off more than we could chew and no amount of heroism could disguise the fact that we were ill-prepared and ill-equipped. Our BEF in Norway was smashed to bits and so shocked was the nation that the defeat was debated in Parliament on May 7th 1940 with far-reaching consequences.

Neville Chamberlain was confident that he could weather the storm because his rival, Winston Churchill, was by no means blameless in the Norway fiasco, but he reckoned without a leading Tory dissident, Leopold Amery, who seized the opportunity to make the speech of his political career by tearing Chamberlain apart, ending with Cromwell's immortal words, 'You have sat too long here for any good you have been doing. Depart, I say, and let us have done with you. In the name of God, go!'

Ironically the man who made a major contribution to Britain's survival by implementing the installation of Winston Churchill as our new leader was also the father of one of our most notorious traitors.

John Amery was the black sheep of this upper-class family whose members had held high office and were held in great esteem throughout the land, but he was a villain and a rebel who spurned the silver spoon and the marvellous opportunities that were available as his birth-right and kicked over the traces.

A number of escapades took him through the courts and at 24 he was adjudged bankrupt with debts of

£5,000. He went to Spain and assisted Franco during the Civil War by gun-running and became involved in Fascism so at the outbreak of World War Two, he went to France where he lived with a young lady member of the Gagoulards (the French fascists) until 1942 when Amery offered his services to the Germans and was invited with his lady friend to Berlin where they registered under the name of Mayer.

He managed to convince Dr Friedrich Hansen, a member of Hitler's personal staff, that he could help Germany's cause and Hansen agreed to become his banker, a decision that caused him considerable consternation as Amery, true to form, indulged in wild spending sprees and charged them all to Dr Hensen.

However, he made several broadcasts to Britain alongside William Joyce (better known to the public as Lord Haw-Haw) but he always saw his main contribution to the German war effort was to raise a force of British soldiers to fight the Russians. They were called the 'British Legion of St George'. This later became the 'British Free Corps' and the men were recruited by Amery and later by other members of the corps by campaigning round the POW camps and offering all kinds of incentives to the weary and hungry prisoners, including a life of luxury, money and unlimited sex, if they would join the cause of Germany and Britain by fighting against communism in the east.

The Duke of Windsor

In spite of all the lies and propaganda and the suggestions that the movement had the support of many top people at home and the flaunting of pictures of ex-King Edward VIII and the statement that they already had 1500 volunteers, the whole enterprise was a complete flop and by the end of the war, in spite of visiting dozens of camps and talking to thousands of POW's, the Free Corps never mustered more than thirty men and these included Canadians, South Africans and Anzacs.

The Germans were at a loss to know what to do with this pitiful handful of drifters, who spent the rest of the war aimlessly awaiting orders which never came and bedding as many frauleins as possible to pass the time away.

When the Russians entered Berlin in 1945 the dedicated anti-communists (with possibly two exceptions) melted away and surrendered to the Allies approaching from the west. Nearly all were tried and given prison sentences varying from three months to life, but the instigator of 'The British Legion of St George' paid the full penalty and was hanged at Wandsworth prison.

John Amery the traitor was 33 years old — so nearly a hero if Hitler had won!

Exit Chamberlain

Chamberlain duly went and on May 10th Winston Churchill took over the reins and as far as I was concerned, not a moment too soon. The Germans were already on the move and true to their form, had crossed the frontiers of neutral Belgium and Holland without any apologies or excuses and before you could say 'Blitzkreig', they were round the Maginot Line and over-running the still ill-equipped British and French troops. By the middle of June a quarter of a million British troops, plus fifty thousand French troops were trapped at Dunkirk and the government were appealing for every small craft available to form a vast fleet and fetch the lads back. The idea appealed to me enor-

mously and I suggested to my father that if he lent me
the fare I could get a train to Dover and lend a hand.

'What do you know about boats?' he demanded.

'Not a lot', I had to admit.

'Then you'd only be in the bloody way', he snorted.
'Now off you go to work!' My future brother-in-law was
one of the last to get out of Dunkirk — sans scarf — and
my sister was hopping up and down with rage: 'To
think some blasted German's wearing it!'

Sid

Soon after Dunkirk came our first close tragedy. My
friend, George, had an elder brother, Sid, who was a
pilot in the RAF. He was 21 and everything our little
gang aspired to. He had a pretty wife and a lovely 18-
month old daughter, a sports car and he looked a million dollars in his uniform, which he very decently let
us all try on for size.

I can still remember posing in it while Sid's favourite
record (Joe Loss playing *Begin the Beguine* with Chick
Henderson singing) made the background music. I still
can't hear that record without thinking of Sid.

On his very first mission he flew to the Dutch coast in
his Blenheim and was never heard of again. It absolutely broke his father, but George was determined to
avenge his brother's death and despite fervant pleas
from the rest of his family, he joined the RAF as an air-
gunner and miraculously survived the war. Yes, he did
get his revenge, but 50 years on I can't help thinking that
there was a German 'Sid' who never came back to his
family. We all thought it was great at the time, but did it
really make everything right?

Invasion Imminent

As soon as our troops were back in 'Blighty' there was a tremendous effort to reorganise our defences and boost the morale of the nation which showed Winston Churchill in his finest role. I doubt if any other man could have picked our nation up by its bootlaces and make us really believe that we could still beat this monster who had captured most of Western Europe and was now sitting just twenty miles away across the Channel.

No one who heard him will ever forget his 'We will fight them on the beaches' speech. He convinced us that we were destined to become heroes as we took up our new role of David, and that we too could beat Goliath. With hindsight I wonder if he believed it himself, for the odds were stacked against us and certainly the American Ambassador, Joseph Kennedy, made no secret of the fact that he thought we were a bad bet and advised President Roosevelt not to get involved. But the important thing was that the British believed Churchill and his dream of a nation of heroes came true.

For the remainder of June there was a lull in the fighting while the Germans regrouped and we licked our wounds, and July was confined to bombing attacks on our coastal convoys and air battles over the Channel. Not until August did the Battle of Britain start in earnest, which had given the RAF vital time to regroup and although they were still well under strength, the new Minister of Aircraft Production, Lord Beaverbrook, was already performing a small miracle by producing more fighters than the RAF were losing. In fact the problem became men more than machines, in spite of the fact that our pilots had every chance of being rescued when they bailed out, whereas the Germans could only expect to be captured, the fact remained that the enemy had been turning out well trained pilots by the thousand, while at the height of the battle our hastily recruited pilots were being thrown in against the Luftwaffe after as little as ten hours training on fighters, as opposed to the original six months' course. Small wonder that many of them were gobbled up by the fanatical German aces before they knew what it was all about.

However, in the face of all adversity the glorious 'Few' emerged triumphant, although the cricket scores of 185 victories in a day proved to be a gross exaggeration for propaganda purposes, they nevertheless hung on until the end of September denying Goering the complete mastery of the air necessary for 'Operation Sealion'. By this time the weather was too unsettled for Hitler to launch his invasion. Britain had reached first base.

The Reichmarshall — Clown or Hero?

Once it was clear that the RAF had given the Luftwaffe a bloody nose the newspaper cartoonists latched on to Goering as a fat figure of fun, not overbright and generally useless. Indeed, an unfortunate fat boy at our youth club who had similar characteristics inevitably received the nickname 'Goering'. It wasn't until after the war that I realised what a lot the Reichsmarshall had going for him. As an army subaltern in the trenches in World War One, he became crippled with arthritis and could hardly walk, yet far from quitting he became one of Germany's most famous fighter pilots, taking over von Richthofen's flying circus and filling the 'Bloody Red Baron's' boots to such good effect that he was awarded the Blue Max. He was a fine horseman and a crack shot and apparently had immense charm and certainly immense courage. If our fat boy at the youth club had known all this, he might even have felt flattered.

The Blitz

Meanwhile we were about to be introduced to 'The Blitz'. On a warm summer's night the warning had gone and we were in the back garden talking to our neighbours over the fence when we were interrupted by two or three collosal bangs and there caught in the searchlights, was our first view of a Heinkel III which twisted and turned and finally escaped, in spite of more collosal bangs from the battery of AA guns at the back of the cemetery. It wasn't until I arrived at work the next morning that I realised that the first bangs we heard was the Heinkel jettisoning its bombs and that it had completely demolished the Alcazar cinema opposite my firm. We spent the entire day sweeping up broken glass and straightening out the cases of type.

This made London realise that we must prepare for the worst and, sure enough, the raids came regularly every night with increasing fury, especially in the docklands and the East End, eventually spreading to the City and then London in general. Edmonton, fortunately, was just outside the main target, but even the 'fringe benefits' were unpleasant.

The Big One

The 7th September, 1940, was 'the big one', for the docks and the surrounding working class districts. Silvertown and Canning Town were particularly hard hit. The Luftwaffe came in as they pleased and queued in orderly fashion to drop their bombs on the target and the fires became out of control in spite of the heroic efforts of the Fire Service and the A.R.P., who were helpless in the face of such fury.

The blaze was so huge that it was quite unapproachable. It lit up the London night sky like an enormous beacon and it was perfectly possible to read a newspaper at midnight ten miles from the centre of the fire.

London's East End had many heroes that night and indeed on many other nights, for the Eastenders were given a hard time for the rest of the Blitz, although the Luftwaffe began spreading its favours around the whole of London and even dropped a bomb on Buckingham Palace a week later which landed in front of the King's study while he was in residence. This made great propaganda for the media that the Royal Family was in the front line with the rest of us.

Underground Death Trap

Those Londoners who did not possess an Anderson shelter discovered a new life-style by spending the night down in the Underground Stations, which seemed a reasonably safe haven deep in the bowels of the earth, but in just over a month four had received direct hits.

The stations were spread right across the Metropolis from Balham and Praed Street to Trafalgar Square and Bounds Green, but by far the worst disaster was at Balham. Nearly seven hundred people were sheltering there when a bomb exploded smashing the gas pipes, the sewerage and the water main and tore through the electric cables. The foul water welled up the emergency stairs and the casualties were enormous. For good measure a double-decker bus sunk up to its rooftop in the hole in the mainshaft of the Underground Station. Hitler was waging total war and the civilians were the number one target!

The Morale Booster

Not surprisingly the terrible holocaust that the bombers were inflicting on the capital night after night began to affect the morale of some of the citizens, and who could blame them when they had seen our troops bedraggled and defeated, scuttling back from Dunkirk and now the apparently invincible Luftwaffe filling the London sky every single night and dropping death and destruction on us at will.

Obviously we needed a sharp reminder that 'Britains never, never, never shall be slaves!' and the last person we should surrender to would be the hated Adolf Hitler. Although Churchill's speeches were inspiring at the time, we needed to believe in ourselves and encourage each other to stand shoulder to shoulder in the desperate struggle for survival.

I was therefore pleasantly surprised when I lifted the copy for my next job at work. It was to be set in bold type and had been handed in by one of the police officers in 'Y' Division and paid for out of his own pocket.

The wording went thus:

'There is no depression in this house and we are not interested in the possibilities of defeat — they do not exist!'

We printed it on white card in blue ink with a red border and everyone in the firm took one home to put on the mantelpiece. The idea spread like wildfire and we printed thousands. I should think half of London had one and it certainly stopped all those moaners in their tracks.

It was fitting that the idea came from a copper, for although they didn't get the glamour treatment that went with a service uniform, hundreds of them risked their lives every night during the blitz with very little recognition, for heroes were two a penny in 1940 — or should I say two for a copper?

'The Grapevine'

We heard of many things on 'the grapevine' for my father was still commuting to Fleet Street and was in the best possible place to know what was happening to our proud and beautiful city and none of the news was good for we were still struggling through our darkest hour. But had we realised it, the mere fact that Goering had stopped bombing our airfields and was concentrating on destroying London was the turning point of the war, for from that day the RAF went from strength to strength and Hitler's Operation Sealion (the invasion of Britain) became a pipe dream.

The impossible had happened and three short months after Hitler had posed in Paris, he was dumbfounded to find that he couldn't cross a twenty mile strip of water to finish us off. By the end of September he ordered his invasion barges to be dispersed and instructed Goering to blow us off the face of the earth.

Chess

Our bedroom had now become the Anderson shelter at the bottom of the garden and it was here that my father introduced me to the rudiments of chess. I soon picked up the basics of the game but my father's idea of chess and mine were poles apart, for while he was pondering three moves ahead, I was busily picking off every available piece in sight, which meant I was finally chasing his lonely king round the board and caused my father to snort with rage, 'you don't play chess — you play bloody draughts!'

The rows got so heated and so regular that my mother eventually put her foot down and banned the chess board from the shelter.

'I don't mind Hitler's bombs', she declared, 'but I can't stand you two playing chess.

We Sink the French Fleet!

With the fall of France a new name had appeared on the leader-board, one General de Gaulle, who caught the public imagination with his spirit of defiance, and I must admit I was pleased to have him on our side. What I didn't know was that for most of the war he was a constant thorn in Winston's flesh, but then there was a whole lot I didn't know about the war until it was over.

Meanwhile Winston had obliterated the French fleet at Oran seeing as the Vichy Government were more likely to lend them to the Germans than to us and de Gaulle had tried to sieze Dakar, an important French port on the West African coast and had retired with egg on his face when the Governor decided he disliked de Gaulle even more than the Germans.

The good news was that Squadron Leader John Oxley had actually led a flight of Hampden bombers in a raid on Berlin which the media made much of. Indeed it was quite a feat for the planes were almost obsolete and a far cry from the Lancasters and Flying Fortresses that would really make Hitler sit up in a year or two, but it severely dented Goering's pride and it certainly made us feel good.

Fire-watching

By this time I had been press-ganged into three firewatch patrols. The first was at the Baptist Church where once a week I was introduced to cards, which later served me in good stead when I was eventually called to the colours.

The second was the firm's patrol which paid three shillings a night and I stood in for the other two compositors twice a week and marvelled that they'd rather be at home than missing all the action. The third was our street patrol and by amazing luck I found I was drawn with 'Babs' a vivacious 17-year old redhead (I was now 17 myself) who lived round the corner.

Came the first patrol and at the appointed hour (2 a.m.) I boldly knocked on Bab's door armed with my stirrup pump and helmet. The door was opened by her father in his pyjamas with a fierce expression on his face.

'And what the bloody 'ell do you want?' he demanded.

'I've come to take Babs firewatching', I said.

'You must be bloody joking!' he replied as he slammed the door in my face. From then on I made do with anyone our leader could get to volunteer, but it was all pretty half-hearted for our plot consisted of two small cul-de-sacs and the portion of Latimer Road that joined them and was only about one hundred yards square, and although there were some near misses, the only incident I can recall was a furious row in the middle of the night between our leader, whose garden backed on to ours, and my father who was strenuously denying that we had an unexploded bomb in our garden while our leader encouraged the A.R.P. to trample all over it.

If it was an unexploded bomb it is still there! Two nights later my father found half of his prize cabbage had disappeared and obviously suspected 'our leader'. It was cut clean in half through the centre but the shrapnel was pretty heavy that night and a large lump of metal travelling at over one hundred miles an hour does weird things, so it remained a mystery.

Mr Jolly's Pigeons

The Blitz was now intruding into the daylight hours and the printers at my firm were downing tools and congregating in the basement as soon as the warning sounded. 'The Guvnor', a Mr Jolly (how can anyone be so misnamed?), stood for this for nearly a week and then came up with 'plan B'.

'I can't pay you for standing around hour after hour doing nothing', he said, 'so when the sirens go I'll take young Dave (yours truly) up on the roof and if we see anything happening we'll blow a whistle.'

This arrangement worked quite satisfactorily for about a fortnight and then while sitting among the chimney pots on this ancient building (circa George III) I spotted some tiny black dots in the sky heading straight for our print shop. Slightly smaller dots were weaving in and out the main body making tack-tack-tack noises. At this point I should explain that the guvnor was extremely hard of hearing, blind in one eye and not too good in the other.

'Look, Mr Jolly!' I cried. 'Planes!'

Old Tom wasn't going to have his men stop work that easily. 'They're not planes, they're bloody pigeons!' he snorted.

This argument was settled by a tremendous whistling noise and within two seconds I had leapt down four flights of stairs, blowing my whistle like crazy. I was only half way down when there was a 'crump' as the bomb exploded two blocks away. I stood at the foot of the stairs in the basement to receive a torrent of abuse from the irate workers who were still at their posts when it went off. Plan B reverted to plan A.

The Dornier

More excitement came the following weekend. We were standing in 'Cockles' garden, the warning had gone but it seemed pretty quiet, when as if from nowhere a Dornier flashed over the roof from a height of no more than two hundred feet, with smoke pouring from one engine.

We were sure it would crash into the allotments at the back and rushed out to catch our first German, but the wretched plane kept on and on still at two hundred feet and disappeared towards Alexandra Palace. We never even had the satisfaction of seeing him crash, although he must have done so eventually — there was no way he could possibly get home.

I consoled myself with the thought that there was plenty of time. The war seemed to have settled down and although we were still being told that there was a very real threat of imminent invasion, I slept easily knowing that Mr Hitler had still got to get across that little strip of water that was guarded by the best Navy in the world. I wouldn't have fancied my chances in a Jerry landing-craft and, of course, if he didn't do it soon, he'd have me to reckon with!

One Old Lady

One fine autumn evening I was standing outside the Baptist Church ready to start my night's firewatch. The warning had not sounded yet, but it was only a matter of time for Goering's lads were in full cry and wouldn't dream of missing a night's fun at our expense.

As a prospective hero I was more than ready to meet the challenge, but as I mentally removed incendiary bombs and held back the flames until the fire brigade arrived, my reverie was broken by the lady attendent from the toilets across the road, tugging at my sleeve. 'I need a big strong lad', she said, 'but you'll do.'

There followed the usual Cockney crosstalk, but I could see that she was worried and followed her to the ladies loos. With some trepidation I went inside with her, feeling not a little embarrassed and then she pointed dramatically, and said, 'I've got a little old lady locked in the end cubicle and I want you to get over the top and let her out!'

I had to be reassured that it wasn't a retake of April Fool's Day or a dummy run of the song about the 'three old ladies who were there from Monday to Saturday', but she demonstrated with her keys that it wouldn't budge, accompanied by a plaintive whining from within, and solomnly handed me a hammer and screwdriver and pushed me into action, having assured me the lady was now decent.

Over the Top

Going over the top took on a whole new meaning as I hoisted myself up and into the cubicle where the occupant was snivelling quietly into her handkerchief. She brightened up considerably once the reinforcements arrived with a few cheerful remarks, not to mention the hammer and I quite enjoyed the next ten minutes smashing away at the errant lock until with a cry of triumph the door burst open to a burst of applause from some half-a-dozen ladies who had come to see what all the excitement was about. For once our hero didn't stop to take an extra bow, I couldn't get out fast enough, pausing only to receive a grateful peck on the cheek from the victim, I was across the road and back in the church just as 'moaning minnie' announced the Luftwaffe was on its way.

It was the East End that was taking the brunt of it —
again, but the noise from the guns made it sound as
though we were in the centre of it. Indeed one of our
dud shells demolished a house in Latymer Road not too
far from our home, but as usual I was elsewhere when
the action started, but at least I'd been a hero of sorts.

Land Mines

We were now becoming familiar with another fiendish
device — the land mine. They were dropped by para-
chute and you could hear them swishing down, which
was bad news for it meant it wasn't going to land too far
away and the damage they did was enormous.

In December 1940 one caught on a lamp-post near the
BBC in Portland Place. It hung there for a minute or so
and then slipped to the ground. The blast demolished
the Langham Hotel and quite a bit of the surrounding
area, but the BBC carried on regardless. Indeed earlier
that evening a smaller bomb had landed on Broadcast-
ing House during the Nine O'clock News and was
heard by thousands of listeners, but the implacable
announcer Bruce Belfrage barely paused before con-
tinuing with business as usual.

War at Sea

During the first two years of the war the U-boats were
having a ball and our shipping losses were enormous,
but there were one or two naval occasions for us to
savour.

The first came quite early in the war when the Ajax,
Exeter and Achilles chased the mighty pocket-battle-
ship, the Grafspee, into Montevideo against far supe-

rior fire power and the German captain scuttled his ship rather than come out and fight. I could well imagine Hitler's fury at this humiliating defeat and perhaps it was just as well the skipper decided to go down with his ship — he'd have been torn to shreds if he'd ever got back to Germany!

The story that pleased me most in the struggle against the U-boats was the tale of the Arandora Star which was plying its way across the Atlantic, bound for Canada, when an Italian submarine on one of its rare sorties into the icy waters north of Ireland, saw her and torpedoed the defenceless merchantman, sending it straight to the bottom.

What the Italian commander didn't know was that the Arandora Star was packed with hardcore Nazis and Italian Fascists bound for internment camps in Canada, and the majority of the prisoners were Italian!

Another candidate for the 'Nearly a Hero' club.

The compositor at work who was my mentor — a cross he bore with a fierce enthusiasm, which led him to lean over the frame and crack me over the head with a sidestick (a tapered piece of wood some three feet long) whenever I disobeyed his instructions — had a dry sense of humour and Frank was never averse to telling a story against himself or his family.

At the height of the U-boats campaign one of their submarines became stranded on the Goodwin Sands and the story became the Page One Splash in all the National newspapers. The Express banner said in huge type 'U-boat on Goodwins'.

Frank's elderly mother was very nearly blind but with an effort she could just make out the splash heading on page one. She came down to breakfast clutching the Express and announced to the family 'U-boats Good Wins' which made Frank choke on his boiled egg and it wasn't until they had wrestled the paper from granny's reluctant hands that they were convinced that Beaverbrook hadn't gone over to the other side.

Any Old Iron

The Boys' Brigade and the Girl Guides had amalgamated to form the nucleus of a Youth Club and encouraged other teenagers to join. 'Cockles' used this as an excuse to chat up every goodlooking girl he met and invite her along, with the implication that he would personally look after her. A promise that proved quite embarrassing when they all turned up at the same time.

When the raids started we used to walk the girls home and on this particular night I had drawn the short straw as escort to a very nice young lady who unfortunately lived near the Roundway, Tottenham and as our club was at Monmouth Road, Edmonton it meant about a seven or eight mile round trip. I successfully saw her home and the raid was building up nicely when I came level with the battery of guns on the Cambridge Arterial Road. At that moment a sergeant major-like voice bellowed an order and the whole jolly lot opened up — it was deafening!

Somewhat shaken I trotted down the Arterial Road for about half a mile to put a reasonable distance between me and the sergeant major's orchestra when I heard the shrapnel whizzing down. As a drowning man clutches at a straw, so I crouched beside a tiny tree only three or four inches wide and held my breath. There was a tremendous crack and a piece of shrapnel smashed into the tree exactly opposite my ear. Enough was enough and I never stopped running until I was back in our Anderson shelter. That night called for a change in tactics for half of the club had been caught out in that raid and it was agreed with all parents that once the warning sounded, we would stay in the shelters wherever we were. Of course in 1940 very few working class people had telephones, so the strain and worry of not knowing where we were must have caused our parents many hours of anxiety, which was quite unnoticed by the Youth Club members who revelled in the excitement of it all.

The ATC

Now that most of my friends were seventeen we all had aspirations to become pilots in the RAF. Indeed my dearest wish was to have a Spitfire for my eighteenth birthday. The Air Training Corps had just started and 1159 Squadron was run by our Boys' Brigade Captain whose other hat was now Squadron Leader.

I was introduced to Trigonometry and Navigation and I was up to ten words a minute in morse and was confident that my Spitfire was in sight. Already half of my friends had got their silver badge to show they had been accepted by the RAF as aircrew and with high hopes I went to Euston to go through the formality. I had never driven a car so the Link Trainer test (a machine which simulated flying a plane) did not go too well, but I was well prepared for the rest and was fairly contented to be told they would take me as an observer (later called navigator) subject to the medical in the afternoon. I was in modern parlance 'over the moon' — the medical was a foregone conclusion. Didn't I win the Wing 880? Didn't I play for the Enfield Battalion football team? Hadn't I won six fights on the trot in the Boxing squad? There was a seventh fight which I shall not dwell on. Sufficient to say a chap named Franks gave me the treatment. Whatever happened to him, I wonder?

My First Setback

So came the medical and it's a piece of cake until . . . until . . . they made me look down a tube with a kind of kaleidoscope at the end, and tell the optician what you see. It was then that the bottom fell out of my world. Apparently my answers didn't agree with the ones on his sheet and to cut a long story short, they offered me a job on the ground staff. I was sick! Didn't they know there was a war on? I politely declined the offer and said that I'd rather go into the navy.

'You'll never get into the navy with your eyes, lad', my tormenter said.

Back I went to 1159 Squadron, the only reject out of some ten or twelve of my particular buddies. I had decided to stay in the ATC until I was called up for there was a week's camp at Hatfield Aerodrome in the offing, and I was still improving my education and my morse was getting pretty good. Plan B — I decided I'd like to be a wireless operator on a submarine!

Hatfield Aerodrome

Sometime in 1941 they got around to registering the first batch of 18-year olds for military service and yours truly was included. I put down for the navy, had a medical and nobody batted an eyelid. Apparently they needed sailors more than aircrews.

Then came our long awaited trip to Hatfield and in spite of being on the Royal Navy's books, I received all the treatment of prospective air crew.

We tried the Link Trainers and I realised that if I could have had that sort of experience before I went to Euston, they would have accepted me as a pilot instead of a navigator before they rejected me.

'Is a rejected pilot more nearly a hero than a rejected navigator?' I asked myself.

Then we were introduced to the Mosquito, which was still on the secret list, for this was the actual home of what was arguably the best and most versatile plane of the whole war — yes, Germans and Yanks included.

We were actually allowed to sit in the cockpit of this fantastic machine and I was torn between delight at the experience and melancholy at the realisation that I would never fly one.

'Cats Eyes Cunningham'

The 'wooden wonder' as it was nicknamed was made mostly from balsa wood which came from Ecuador and as around seven thousand Mosquitos were built by the end of the war, the effect on their balsa forest must have been devastating.

The idea of the plane was dreamed up at Salisbury Hall near St Albans, which is just a hop down the road from Hatfield, by Sir Geoffrey de Havilland and C.C. Walker, and by 1941 they had still not convinced the Air Ministry that this star of the future was worth persevering with, although the officer who showed us around told us that 'Cats Eyes Cunningham', the night fighter pilot who could see in the dark, reputedly because he ate carrots (no-one had yet revealed that we now had radar) had switched from his usual Beaufighter and tried out this very Mosquito and as a night fighter he was extremely impressed.

Indeed he was so impressed that he flew Mosquitos for the rest of the war.

A whole cottage industry grew up around Hatfield, making vital parts for the plane which was to become an intruder bomber, photographic reconnaisance, a nightfighter, an escort for mass bomber raids and a pathfinder as well.

My First Flight

The Air Ministry may not have had a very high opinion of the Mosquito in 1941 but Goering thought sufficiently highly of Hatfield as early as 1940 to bomb it. A JU88 hit the sheet metal shop and the Technical School with four bombs before it was shot down. Twenty-one workers were killed and seventy were injured.

The German pilot was captured and recognised as a former pupil at the Technical School and he obviously knew the true worth of Hatfield. A further 68 bombs were dropped around the locality but the precious prototype of the Mosquito was unscathed.

How much harder it would have been for the RAF if they had been deprived of this magnificent aeroplane one can only imagine.

The highlight of our week was a trip in a Tiger Moth. It was my first flight and the Sergeant-Pilot took a great delight in giving us cadets the works. Through the intercom he asked me whether I wanted to loop-the-loop and while I was still thinking of a way to decline without appearing 'chicken', he took my silence for consent and enthusiastically turned the whole world upside down. I shut my eyes and wasn't too sorry I was going into the navy — or perhaps I'd have settled for a Wellington instead of a Spitfire.

Still Unprepared

Back to civvy street and still no call-up, and in spite of the fact that we now had Russia and the USA on our side, things were still looking pretty black. Just as in the early days of the war, the Germans had walked all over us, so were the Japs giving the Yanks the same treatment with no holds barred. Did someone mention Pearl Harbour?

Nor were we any more ready for them than the Americans, in spite of having already been at war for more than two years. Our lack of preparation in Singapore will live forever in the annals of shame, when a much smaller number of Japs marched straight in the back door and took our so-called impenetrable fortress in a matter of days. 'Lions led by donkeys' was never a more apt description of our troops and for good measure the Prince of Wales and the Repulse, two of our finest battleships had been sent out to meet the Japs without any air support, and were completely helpless against the Japanese bombers who could hardly believe their luck as they gratefully sank them.

We were still learning the hard way.

It must have been a great relief to Winston in the face of all this adversity when I wrote in and reminded the navy that I had registered three months ago and wasn't it about time they realised their assets? I could imagine the PM confiding to a packed House, 'All is well, they've called up David Windsor!'

Butlin's Navy

I reported to HMS Royal Arthur, which sounded very nautical but turned out to be Billy Butlin's holiday camp at Skegness. They still had the sign over the entrance which said, 'Our true intent is your delight', but apparently the Chief at the gate couldn't read for in ten seconds flat he was giving us an earful which I didn't find at all delightful.

The next day we were kitted out and were given an aptitude test. We filled in a form which enquired what we wished to be. The joker I had palled up with put down 'Admiral', but the Chief didn't think it was all that funny.

Determined to get into action I stated that I could do around 14 words a minute at morse and I wanted to be a telegraphist on a submarine. Had I realised the perverse way in which the navy interprets your wishes I would have applied for a position as a clerk in the Wrens and probably finished up on a Murmansk convoy.

Special Sparks

However, eventually I arrived in a room with 30 or 40 other recruits and we soon found we were all classified as Telegraphists SO. There was much speculation as to the meaning of the classification 'S.O.', and my pal Johnny the Joker was happy to explain it to them.

Pointing at me he said he's put in for the Submarines, so that stands for 'Submarines Only'.

This caused considerable consternation among the assembly and a certain amount of hostility towards myself as though it was all my fault, for at least half of them were less than enthusiastic about being called to the colours, let alone spending the rest of the war in a sub, always assuming the sub lasted till the end of the war.

Enter the Chief to be bombarded with the 64,000 dollar question — 'What does the S.O. stand for?' 'It stands for Special Operator', said the Chief and paused dramatically and surveyed us with an enigmatic smile (a habit which later earned him the nickname of 'Mona'). Johnny was in straight away — 'Does that mean we'll be landing commandos or spies?' he asked.

'No, it means that they think you lot are brighter than the average stoker, indeed some of you might have an I.Q. of 2 or even 3, so you're going to become experts in foreign morse'. We then had to indicate whether we wanted to go to sea, or overseas or home service, but already my sub had sunk without a trace.

Buns and Cocoa

We were now in a class and started our basic training and a lad named Nixon from Crawley was made class leader by the Chief because he'd been in the Home Guard and couldn't keep it to himself. . . . 'And some have greatness thrust upon them'.

He took his responsibilities quite seriously but unfortunately the only status he had was that if anything went wrong, he carried the can. The mornings were 'bracing' as they say in Skegness and by the time we had completed our PT and followed this by a run round a distant windmill, we were ready for our mid-morning break which consisted of buns and cocoa which went by the extraordinary name of 'Pussa Kye', phonetically speaking of course. As the doors of Princes dining hall were opened, we rushed to our mess tables and there was a mad scramble with every man for himself.

Our leader was mortified. 'Look at 'em', he snorted. 'Bloody animals!' He glared at the seething mass of humanity struggling round the buns and cocoa. 'It will be different tomorrow, I promise you!' As good as his word the next morning he was at the forefront of the still seething mass of humanity and was first through the doors and first at the table. He flung his arms across the buns and shouted, 'Stop! Form a queue.'

Unfortunately we were issued with forks with which to eat the buns and as the tidal wave rushed in, every man jack was trying to spear his bun, and it appeared our leader was getting more than his fair share of the fork prongs. Within seconds his hands had been punctured in countless places and with the blood welling out rapidly, he disappeared in the direction of the sick bay. Somebody obligingly ate his bun to save it from being wasted.

If The Cap Fits. ..

Skegness was not at its best in 1942. Most of the shops seemed to sell fish and chips but there's more to life than touring fish and chip shops. The Saturday night dance produced about five girls and a hundred or so matelots, plus a similar number of 'erks' from the RAF, so the bar was pretty busy.

At the end of the evening I took my cap off the rack and sauntered out into the blackout with Johnny. We'd gone about twenty yards when there was a patter of running feet and we heard a voice crying, 'Jack, Jack!'

Another rookie matelot came sprinting up and said in broad Cockney, 'You've got me 'at, mate'. I took mine off and examined the identical one he was proffering. They were both new, both the same size and both had an HMS cap tally. 'How do you know?' I asked.

'Because me french letter's tucked inside it, and me girl's waiting up the road', he replied.

Next morning we strolled along the front and perused the hotels where the RAF were billeted. 'Lucky bleeders', said Johnny, 'they've really got it made'. We had almost got back to camp when the Dornier came in low from the sea and straddled the hotels with a stick of bombs causing a great many RAF casualties.

'Lucky bleeders?' I asked Johnny, and for once he was lost for words.

Not So Dusty

Our chief tormenter was a Petty Officer named 'Dusty' Miller — all Millers are nicknamed 'Dusty' in the navy. His claim to fame was that he was the only sane person aboard and to prove it he'd got a clearance certificate when they had let him out of the looney bin. True or false, we could certainly believe it of him.

He gave us merry hell, but he certainly knocked us into shape. Nothing personal unless you upset him, and woe betide the man who did. There was a Norwegian to whom he took a particular dislike and the feeling was mutual, but the Chief held all the aces and tormented him unmercifully until finally the Viking could take no more. With a roar he rushed at 'Dusty' with his fixed bayonet and chased him round the square until he was finally overpowered by the MP's. It didn't do the Norwegian much good — he got 90 days in the brig, but it didn't do much for 'Dusty's' reputation either.

It's All Greek

Royal Arthur was full of foreign sailors from all the occupied countries, but I particularly remember the Greeks. They used to play childlike games in the bar with tremendous enthusiasm. In their favourite game, the one who was 'it' faced the wall with his hands behind his back, palms facing outward, then one of his mates would creep up and slap his hand as hard as he could. Simultaneously the rest would crowd round him with their fingers pointing in the air and hissing.

The victim had to pick out the culprit and if he guessed right they swapped places. You could be there a long time before you guessed right. Childish it was, but it was also great fun and it helped them forget the troubles of their beloved homeland.

The Dome and St Dunstans

At the end of our basic training we were sent to Brighton for a couple of months to learn the rudiments of morse which, with my ATC training, was an absolute doddle so that I was able to concentrate on the more serious things in the town, like 'the Dome' and Sherries Bar.

The first day we arrived the CO gave us a pep talk on the merits of HMS Vernon and told us that Sherries Bar was an undesirable establishment where there was always trouble and dubious ladies, so naturally we could hardly wait to get there. Half the men on the course had already completed their first month so naturally they showed us the ropes.

The course incidentally was conducted at St Dunstan's Home for the Blind, and I could not help but reflect that if the RAF had not suggested that I was half blind, I wouldn't be here at St Dunstans.

It was only ninepence for the forces to get into the Dome, which was the most popular dancehall in town, but as our pay was only tenpence a day we still had a problem. This was solved by the girls who were friends of the first draft, pooling their pass-out tickets and one of them slipping out and distributing them to us — now we could afford a drink as well!

Higgins the Provider

In spite of our financial embarrassment we lived pretty well. Soon after our arrival in Brighton a pal of mine named Jack Higgins suggested that we went out that

evening for a drink. I asked the obvious question —
'What do we use for money?' and he just winked and
said, 'trust me'.

With some trepidation I accompanied him into town
and we looked in at several pubs before he finally said,
'this will do'. We boldly strode up to the bar and spent
our combined capital on two halves of bitter. His next
move was to carry them over to a battered piano in the
centre of the bar and, pushing his cap flat aback on his
head, he started to play. He was brilliant!

I was brought up on sing-songs round the piano and
in no time at all the joint was jumping and miraculously
the top of the piano began to fill up with pints.

Higgins beamed 'drink up' and we had the time of
our lives. We had the good sense to restrict it to twice a
week, and never used the same pub twice running.

'Keep 'em wanting more', said Higgins.

Tommy Farr's Bar

I was sitting in the gods at the Grand Theatre one night
when a beefy man of about 40 sat down beside me and
in the interval introduced himself as a local butcher,
which brought forth the inevitable pun that at least he
could make both ends meat. He didn't get it, but he did
buy me a beer and I settled down to enjoy the second
half of the show. As we were filing out after the final
curtain, he suggested 'one for the road', which sounded
like an offer I couldn't refuse and he introduced me to
Tommy Farr's Bar.

We had barely sat down when two hefty Canadians
barged in, obviously the worse for drink and started to
make a right nuisance of themselves. Suddenly the
curtains at the back of the bar parted and a figure with

shoulders the width of a barn door appeared. Tommy tucked one drunk under each arm as though they were children and hurled them out into the gutter.

The Leer

Joe Louis and co had made such a mess of his eyes that he was unfit for military service which I thought was a great pity because on that performance he could have handled the entire German army on his own.

It soon became apparent that my Brighton butcher wasn't buying the beer because of the grand job I was doing in the Royal Navy. He began complimenting me on my physique and his smile was becoming a leer, and then he suggested we went back to his place to finish off a bottle of rum.

I didn't argue. He led the way out of the pub and turned left out of the door and I turned sharp right and disappeared into the blackout.

I can still hear his plaintive cry of 'Jack! Jack! Where are you?'

Rommel

A new German general had arrived in North Africa and soon became a household name — even Churchill grudgingly admired Erwin Rommel and his first important success was to capture Torbruk in Libya and give our own General Auchinleck a lesson in desert warfare, which led to Winston flying out to Egypt and sacking all his desert generals and a new star was born. I give you Bernard Montgomery — 'Monty' to you.

At last the Brits had a soldier hero!

Bully-Off

It was at Brighton that I first experienced the class bully. Up to now I'd had a pretty trouble-free ride, for I mixed fairly easily and was fit enough to survive, but being rather on the short side I must have seemed fair game for anyone over six feet that felt like throwing his weight about.

There was one particular thug named Thresher who left a trail of mayhem wherever he went, although he made a point of avoiding the other ratings who were six feet plus unless they were designed like a bean pole in which case they got the same treatment as us lesser mortals.

My turn came eventually. We were queuing in the canteen at tea-break when he pushed in front of me in the queue. Not surprisingly I asked him to explain his conduct — or words to that effect — whereupon he whipped round and gave me a hefty dig in the solar plexus which really knocked the wind out of me. By the time I'd got my breath back he'd taken his tea and bun and disappeared.

Time for Action

I now had a problem. If I ignored it he would treat me like dirt for evermore, as indeed he was already doing to several of the lads, but in a straight fight I had every chance of being eaten alive.

The whistle blew telling us to fall in for the rest of the morning's classes and as we began to form our squads I decided it was time for action. That punch in my abdomen may have knocked the stuffing out of me, but it had also made me so mad I couldn't care less about the consequences.

Thresher was shaping up in the back row of his squad and had already forgotten me as one would dismiss a fly you had brushed off your shoulder. Me, I was still livid with rage and determined to level the score.

The gardener had just hoed the flower beds and they were covered with a fine tilth which gave me the solution in a flash. I scooped up a large handful of earth and just as the parade was called to order by the Chief I pulled back his dickey collar and stuffed it down the back of his neck and in the same movement fell in on the end of the line.

Collision Course

Short of whining to the Chief that he had been attacked by someone at least eight inches shorter than he was, there was nothing Thresher could do except wriggle in discomfort until the parade was dismissed. To say I was apprehensive was something of an understatement but the die was cast and I was determined to give as good as I got, not necessarily in a toe to toe punch-up, more a knee into his vitals at the opportune moment.

Sure enough, I passed my adversary in the corridor at the end of the morning session and I braced myself as we walked towards each other on a collision course. As he came nearer I decided to keep it simple and to kick him straight in the shins at the first sign of trouble, but to my relief and amazement he strode straight past looking clean over the top of me, and we never exchanged a word between us from that day on.

There were side benefits to this episode, for the word got around that 'you don't mess around with Windsor', and nobody went out of their way to give me a hard time from that very day.

Canadian Capers

Our civvy billet was half filled with Canadian soldiers and we got on pretty well with them in spite of their inflated pay packets. It was one of those stupid things that on the odd occasion there was a flare up in the Dome between the Brits and the Canadians, usually over a girl and, although I was never averse to a punch-up, I couldn't see the point of doing Hitler's job for him and I steered clear of it.

Indeed it was a Canadian that found me my regular girl friend while I was in Brighton. As I came out of Sherry's Bar he was strolling along with a girl on each arm. 'Do you want a hand?' I asked jokingly. 'Come aboard, Jack', he replied — and that was how I met Doreen.

She was beautifully designed and very good company and soon she was asking all the usual questions, where I came from (a blind man could have guessed I came from London) and how old I was. When I admitted to being nearly nineteen, her face dropped a little. 'You're only a boy!' she cried. 'I am twenty one'. To which I replied, 'I may be only a boy, but I could cause you a lot of trouble'. She laughed at that and we had six or seven weeks of great fun together before I moved on.

I never wrote. I knew she would have other boy friends before we met again and there didn't seem much point. In wartime you live one day at a time.

My Landlady and the Fiddler

My other recollections of Brighton were of our landlady who was a bit of a dragon but fully qualified to make her present strange guests toe the line. She had a love-hate relationship going with the sole civilian guest, a middle-aged violinist named Vic who 'scraped' a living in the orchestra pit at the Grand. (It was he who provided my ticket which led to my escapade with the Brighton butcher.) But I digress. . .

We used to speculate if wedding bells were in the offing, but mostly the bells signified the start of the next round.

I must mention our daily smile as we walked to St Dunstans passing the pie shop en route. Three or four girls worked near the window making the pies and as there was a paper shortage, the manager was appealing to his clients to save paper. Hence the notice stuck on the window, 'It takes a bag to make a pie!'

Farewell Brighton, Hello Eastbourne

We were now up to twenty words a minute at morse and time to move on to Eastbourne for a month or so to be transformed into 'Special Operators'. There I was introduced to the codes and call signs of the German and Italian navies, with particular emphasis on submarines, while our colleagues in the other half of the class were taught Japanese morse, again with the emphasis on subs.

Higgins was in the Japanese half but we managed a couple of good 'runs ashore' during that mojth.

The previous draft had only a couple of days left before they finished their course, but they took us to the Winter Gardens and dutifully handed over their girl friends, as we would do in turn to the next draft at the end of the month.

By an amazing coincidence one of them was a girl from my youth club who was now serving in the WAAFS. My determination to get at Hitler faltered and I could cheerfully have spent the rest of the war in Eastbourne.

St Bedes and the Gorbals

We did our studies at St Bedes (yes, I know it's a girl's college), beautifully situated on the cliff tops near Beachy Head. Every morning we marched from our billets on the front, along the coast road and at halfway we were always passed by a nurse cycling in the opposite direction to town. She always waved and we chorused 'Morning nurse' as numerous matelots before and after us had done.

At lunch break we would sit on the lawns at St Bedes and often watch our fighters streaming out across the Channel to intercept the Luftwaffe and I felt sick with discontent, but I consoled myself with the thought that I had nearly finished my training, then it would be my turn.

The only man in our outfit who doubted we would get a turn was a character named 'Jock' May who assured us that the war couldn't last much longer because he'd never kept a job for more than six months. He had a rare sense of humour, but apparently he'd been a member of a notorious razor gang in the Gorbals, and he would sit on the edge of his bunk at night practising 'the scissors' and various other strokes that were part of his trade. I never stood near Jock when he was shaving.

In May 1994 I was in Eastbourne on business and revisited St Bedes which had changed beyond all recognition. Every Naval Establishment has a ship's name and looking through my certificate of service, I am reminded that St Bedes was Victory III, which seemed appropriate for the school which had come through perils of the Luftwaffe raids unscathed and had become a triumph for the British educational system. I was taken on a guided tour and was amazed at the improvements which had taken place. They have added a swimming pool, extended the chapel and added several extensions, but the jewel in the crown is the magnificent sports hall which not only caters for most indoor sports, including tennis, but also doubles as a concert hall. 1995 is their centenary year and the other piece of information I gathered is that the joker who told us it was a girl's college was just winding us up!

On a topical note, they told me that they still turn up the odd unexploded bomb now and then. I can imagine the German pilot reporting that he had dropped his bombs on England — just!

Chatham

It was time to leave Eastbourne and we stowed our kitbags aboard a couple of lorries and proceeded to HMS Pembroke (Chatham Barracks to you) where we were greeted by the inevitable previous draft, all of them sporting their telegraphists badges as their new status symbol. This time there were no social introductions for girl friends were at a premium in that neck of the woods, with several hundred matelots to every local lass, so we made for 'the smoke' which the uninitiated call London. The fare was 1/9d return to London Bridge, so I dug deep into my pocket and spent the weekend with the family and paid a flying visit to the now sadly depleted youth club.

The news wasn't good. Three of the lads had bought it, including Frank who was a particular friend of mine. His Wellington had been shot clean out of the sky, so at least the end was quick, and another lad 'Richie' who was in my platoon in the Boys' Brigade had been lost at sea.

To cap it all I met Bert the delivery boy at the printshop as I was walking down the High Street and gleefully offered him my hand, only to be proffered an awkward left hand. His right sleeve was dangling empty and pinned to his chest. I was mortified.

The Tunnel

We slept in 'the tunnel' at Chatham. It was like an Anderson shelter that went on for ever. The night we arrived we were absolutely shattered, so by nine o'clock we made a beeline for our new bedroom, slung our hammocks from the hooks and I sank into a dreamless sleep. I was awakened at six a.m. by a terrible racket as two Petty Officers roared through the tunnel dragging their batons along the corrugated iron and screaming, 'Wakey wakey, rise and shine!' I sat up sharply in my hammock and crashed my head into the hammock which had been slung a mere eighteen inches above mine.

The entire shelter was a vast cocoon of hammocks as far as one could see, and you could cut the air with a knife, but with the Luftwaffe still a force to be reckoned with, it made sense to keep this vast reserve of trained men out of harm's way.

After all our months of intense training we felt like fish out of water at Chatham. We were found pathetic jobs to do and told to look busy until we were drafted. They tell of one pair of 'barrack stanchions' (a nickname for part of the building) who spent half the war carrying a ladder between them to nowhere in particular until it was time to go ashore.

Some of our lads enjoyed it and said it was better than a draft chit, but personally I was champing at the bit to get on with my 'Special Operations' and was painfully aware that the previous draft was still in Chatham.

The Premature Draft Chit

It was then with typical naval mismanagement that it all happened. We had been in Chatham less than two weeks when they decided they were ready to dispatch the next batch of telegraphists overseas, and the clerk seeing our little lot on his books, completely overlooked the previous bunch and issued our draft chits.

The others were helpless with laughter and even helped us hurl our kitbags into the lorry as we headed off into the great unknown. What a send-off they gave us! You'd have thought we were going on a victory march through Berlin instead of picking up their draft chitties by mistake.

Our lorries dumped us at King's Cross Station where we were given two hours' leave and told not to speak to anyone about our draft. We would have had a job to tell anyone anything, for although our tropical kit was showing all over the place, we hadn't the faintest idea where we were going, although it obviously wasn't Scapa Flow.

Two hours would have just been enough for me to have gone home to Edmonton and said 'Hi' and about turned and come back again, but travel was far too uncertain to take that chance and I don't think it would have particularly cheered my mother up to see that I was off for real this time, so I joined a couple of friends and went into a local pub where a middle-aged suicide blonde (died by her own hand) was pouring her heart out into a mike accompanied by a one man band.

One of our lads was a right country bumpkin from deepest Norfolk who had rarely been beyond his village until he was called up and frankly confessed that a big city like Brighton frightened him, and here he was as he put it 'in the heart of London's night life'. We didn't disillusion him and indeed he never saw anything more sophisticated than the pub at King's Cross until the war was over.

The Convoy Assembles

Our two hours was up and we were bundled into a train that shuffled and shunted through the night until the following day we arrived at Lime Street Station in Liverpool, all without disembarking. Just try to book a similar journey these days and you'd be stymied at the booking office.

Amid great excitement we boarded a New Zealand meat ship 'The Rangitikei' which was moored opposite the Liver Buildings and for a whole day we watched the Birkenhead ferry ply to and fro while the convoy assembled.

The naval contingent being used to the sea (they must be joking) were down in the bowels of the fore castle. There were seventeen on our mess deck in a space of about six feet by fourteen feet where we had to live, eat and sleep.

Slinging your hammocks was like Chatham tunnel all over again, only this time there was a very real danger that the chap above you would, to use a naval term, 'spew his ring up'. We had two or three that had a really bad time, but they never came below deck which saved the rest of us from joining them.

As we ploughed through the Irish Sea heading out past Scotland the heads on deck became awash with troops retching miserably. The naval ratings were given duties on board the ship and I found this helped me ignore its perverse antics as it rolled, pitched and tossed in a world of grey sea mingling with grey sky and then again grey sky mingling with grey sea. I was determined not to embarrass myself or show myself up while wearing my naval uniform, although I came very near to it when I had to deliver a message to the RAF's mess. The whole place was awash with vomit and the stench was horrific. How those airmen must have longed for an airfield.

The Canaries

We went far out into the Atlantic to avoid the U-boats which were operating from St Nazaire and other French ports and eventually cut back to the Canary Islands which, being Spanish and therefore neutral, were ablaze with lights — the first I'd seen since 1939, but of course, our convoy was still in complete darkness and it was a source of amazement to me how the same dirty tramp that was alongside us off our starboard bow at sunset was still in exactly the same place at dawn.

I was enjoying the trip immensely, as though I was on a holiday cruise. There were constant pontoon schools in operation with no limit and I soon discovered that by betting a shilling on a card until I was dealt an ace and then betting a fiver, the odds were well in my favour, notwithstanding the inevitable disaster now and then. Beer was fourpence halfpenny a pint (just over tuppence in new money). The sun shone as we steamed south and day after sun-soaked day I lived like a king as we sailed through those tropical waters and when we finally disembarked I was the magnificent sum of £34 richer — or to put it into perspective, nearly ten month's pay better off!

Entertainment for the Troops

In the afternoons there were impromptu concerts held in the well deck with troops of all denominations crowded round helping the proceedings along. At the first one, after we had been at sea three or four days, a matelot sang the ballad of the River Plate to the tune of South of the Border. The whisper went round that he was a survivor off the Exeter and he received tumultous applause.

He sang it again on the second day and again on the third, by which time the applause was muted. On the fourth day he was halfway through his rendition when a squadie tossed a penny which landed at the performer's feet.

Contemptuously he picked it up and heaved it over their heads and into the briny and called out in a loud voice, 'Come down the man who threw that copper coin! I'll fight him m'self.' 'And me', cried his mate who had three goes at Red River Valley. 'And me'. 'And me' echoed his oppos and in no time at all there was a struggling mass of humanity in the well deck.

Providently eight bells sounded and most of the matelots had to answer a higher call, yours truly included, or they would still have been fighting when we reached our first port of call which was Freetown, the capital of Sierra Leone.

Freetown Harbour

This was my first introduction to a foreign port, for until I joined the navy I'd never even crossed the Channel, and I suppose this was probably true of 90% of British servicemen. Most of them had worked five and a half or six days a week, and only the lucky ones got a fortnight's holiday which they spent at a seaside resort within a fifty mile's radius of their homes. So the sight of Freetown Harbour with all its bustling activity was tremendously exciting.

It is a very deep, very large, natural harbour which made it an ideal service station for the convoys plying to the Far East or even the Middle East, for at this stage of the war the Axis had control of France, Italy and Sicily and still had a hold in North Africa, so convoys through the Mediterranean with overcrowded troop-ships were a last resort and had to be sent round the Cape of Good Hope. Hence the vital importance of Freetown.

We had barely heaved to when a flotilla of 'bum-boats' set out from the shore and made a beeline to-wards us, all manned by jet black natives clad in only a loin cloth and many were direct descendants of West African slaves.

There were two types of boatmen, the traders and the entertainers. The first had fruit for sale, much of which would have started a queue a mile long in war-torn England. There were bananas, oranges, lemons, melons and even pineapples, and soon there was a brisk trade by means of a basket lowered over the side with the money in it and the fruit being hauled back up.

It was a tricky business, for neither side trusted the other. The bum-boat could sail away with the money or the troops could pull the fruit up and disappear inside the ship, but usually it was money first.

Glasgow Tanner

Meanwhile the entertainers were shouting 'Dive for Glasgow Tanner' to the troops and someone would toss a shining sixpence over the side and the young lads would dive off their canoe into the filthy water to fetch it.

The first time I saw this exercise I thought, 'What a waste of sixpence!' for it seemed impossible to find anything in that murky harbour, but just when I thought he must have drowned, he emerged triumphant holding the coin in his hand. He must have had lungs like a pearl diver. Sometimes the intrepid divers would surface cursing the donator who had thrown a genuine Glasgow tanner, which was a farthing covered in silver paper, while the troops hanging over the side chanted, 'You win some, you lose some'.

The flotilla was eventually dispersed because the bartering system had broken down and a furious squaddie and an equally furious West African were calling each other 'thieving baskets'.

The argument was settled by the simple expedient of turning the ship's hose on the bum-boats and scattering them in all directions, which they seemed to accept as the inevitable end to the day's trading. It seemed a method we could well use as a fitting climax on our own Stock Exchange.

Flying Ants

Here we parted company with our friends who had been learning Japanese morse. They were going on to Trincomalee via South Africa, which made even the Japanese morse seem worthwhile. The rest of us were told to disembark, and we strode down the gang plank straight into a plague of flying ants. These one-winged insects swarmed in their millions all over us.

It was horrible, but as we fought our way through them to the waiting lorries, they suddenly fell dying to the ground, completely covering the floor with a black and silver carpet.

What a relief! We were all firmly convinced that this was the norm in Africa and we couldn't begin to imagine life in a place with ants permanently in your hair and your mouth — and as for eating, it didn't bear thinking about!

In fact it happens about once a year, and we had to pick that day to arrive.

The Top Hat

We piled into the two waiting lorries and set off into darkest Africa. As we slowed down going through a small village, a weird character wearing a top hat appeared and thumped on the side of the lorry, demanding money.

His exact words were 'You dash me Johnny' and on being told to go away — or words to that effect — he became quite abusive and started lashing out with a stick. As he came level with me I leaned over the side and rammed his hat over his eyes as hard as I could.

Our driver got the message and sped off into the dusk and by the time our friend had got his top hat off, the second lorry had just gone past him and the startled occupants were amazed to see a lunatic in a top hat running down the road screaming abuse and hurling rocks at them.

HMS Aberdeen

The lorries dropped us off at HMS Aberdeen, which was a collection of nissen huts near the seaside surrounded on three sides by a mangrove swamp. We fell in and were inspected by the CO, a South African regular, who welcomed us and then gently informed us that this hellhole was to be our home for the next eighteen months! In the event it was nearly two and a half years, but who's counting?

My mouth dropped. We'd thought at least we would be joining the Freetown escort, which were mostly river-class frigates escorting the convoys between Gibraltar and Lagos.

The CO explained patiently, as he probably had to every previous draft, that our job was far too important to allow us to go frigging about on frigates in the Freetown escort. We were experts (or would be in a very short while) who were going to save thousands of tons of merchant shipping in both the North and South Atlantic from the menace of the U-boat, and with Germany turning out a sub a day, they needed all the help they could get.

I wasn't convinced, I felt sure that any merchant seaman would rather have a frigate between him and the U-boats than know I knew exactly where they were, but this was the CO's welcoming speech, not a debating society.

The Monsoons

He concluded by congratulating us because we'd arrived at the start of the monsoon season, which although rather wet, was preferable to the height of summer, when the temperature rose to 120 degrees or more and the water supply tended to run out. On these occasions we would be rationed to one milk bottle of water a day which we could either wash with or slake our thirst. I still can't bear to see a tap running for no purpose to this day.

However, for the moment the problem was exactly the reverse. The rain came down in buckets, the like of which I had never seen in dear old Blighty. The ramshackle mud huts of the natives were washed clean off the hillsides and in Freetown the gutters, which were six feet deep became raging torrents and woe betide any drunk that staggered out of the bars on a dark night. Once they had tripped into the gutter, they were washed away and their bodies fished out the next day or even disappeared for ever. It seemed a stupid way to die when they'd done all that training, travelled thousands of miles and never got around to firing a shot in anger.

But I digress (again) for the CO, having felt he had done enough, handed over to Jimmy the One who explained in more detail that our job was to listen to U-boat frequencies and when one popped up, to take a bearing on it. These were compared with other stations in the South Atlantic and where the bearings crossed, there was your U-boat.

We could even get bearings on subs in the North Atlantic and many a night the air was thick with 'B-bars' and 'E-bars' which signalled that a U-boat had sighted a convoy and was calling in the rest of the pack.

It was exciting, but irksome at the same time. It wasn't my idea of what the navy was all about and I thought ruefully that I would probably have seen more action with the RAF ground staff.

Tokyo Rose

We resigned ourselves to regular watchkeeping seven days a week (our day off started when you came off the morning watch at eight a.m.) month after month, indeed year after year. We often listened to two frequencies at once — one in each ear, but if you were lucky and only had one station to monitor you could tune into 'Tokyo Rose' on the other.

She sounded like a million dollars but her propaganda could certainly get under your skin if you let it. She was not slow to point out that the Yanks were now in England in large numbers, while most of the Brits had been sent overseas. 'And who do you think is looking after your wives and girlfriends?' she would enquire in a sad voice. She had a point and I felt truly thankful that I hadn't left a steady girlfriend behind.

She always closed with the quotes 'Good morning to some of you, good afternoon to some more of you, and to the rest of you, goodnight'. All this in the sexiest voice imaginable and you could look round the operations room and identify those who were mentally climbing into bed with Tokyo Rose.

Gus-Gus

There were a dozen of us in our nissen hut, starting with Mac the killick who was in charge, my two particular buddies, Benny and Bugsy, and the camp extrovert who went by the unlikely name of Augustus Gusher which inevitably earned him the nickname of 'Gus-Gus'.

He was terribly earnest and sincere and always gave 200% into whatever he was 'enjoying' at the time. Whatever activity was available Gus-Gus was right there having a go. To me he personified the quotation 'the road to hell is paved with good intentions' for he lived in a perpetual maelstrom of his own making. He was a keep fit fanatic with a waist line of twenty inches which sloped up to extremely wide shouders and his whole body was simply rippling with muscles — even his muscles had muscles (which gave him another nickname of 'Musclebound').

Unfortunately, he had a face like a weasel and a squint which put him slap bang back among the also-rans when it came to pulling the birds. The first thing 'Gus-Gus' did when he settled in was to acquire a soapbox to put alongside his bunk, to put his few possessions in and he topped it with a photo of his regular girlfriend in Brighton. We winced when we saw it for we recognised her as 'the camp bike' — everyone had a ride on her! However, we let it pass but unfortunately, every new draft that came out had someone who said 'I've been with her!' Eventually Mac asked him to keep it out of sight as he was getting fed up with the punch-ups.

The Carpenter

Benny, Bugsie and myself were all keen on boxing and together with a couple of others we formed a boxing squad and, of course, Gus-Gus wanted part of the action. It soon became obvious that fit as he was, he wasn't the world's greatest boxer, but he had enormous courage and would never lie down. Benny with his inimitable direct approach, suggested to all and sundry — and Gus in particular as he was wiping his bloody nose — that it would be best if he left the squad as we were fed up with beating him up.

However, we weren't averse to handing out the same treatment to the natives who saw themselves as the next Joe Louis, except that none of them had ever seen a real set of boxing gloves before, let alone put them on. Just like a fairground booth at home, we used to line up outside the mess and offer twenty cigarettes (a small fortune to them) to anyone who could beat us — take your pick.

Being only five feet six inches tall I was a popular choice and it came as no surprise when the camp carpenter who was built like an ox and stood over six feet pointed his grubby finger at me. It was a bit worrying because no one had actually won a packet of fags yet, and I didn't want to be the first to let the side down.

He strutted round in the dust (we didn't have a ring, just a crowd of onlookers) and then suddenly he put his head down and charged. I sidestepped smartly and thumped his ear as he roared past, to loud applause from my shipmates and screams of annoyance from the Timni and Mendi tribesmen on the opposite side of the ring. Five times he made the identical move and five times I evaded him and thumped his head.

Just as he was about to make a sixth charge, he had a better idea. He ripped off the gloves and grabbed a chain that was hanging round his waist and yelling like a zulu warrior he rushed at me again with arms akimbo intent on putting the chain round my throat. Obviously the chap had never heard of the Queensberry Rules and I hadn't the time to explain them to him. I ducked past the flaying chain and smartly stuck out my foot and he fell flat on his face. As one man the rest of the squad jumped on him and seized the chain. The place was in an uproar and it was fortunate that 'Jimmy the One', an officer with a rare sense of humour, was just passing and his presense was enough to break it up.

Explanations followed and that was the end of our fairground boxing booth, but no one was punished and we reverted to boxing each other.

The Focke Wolf Condor

We had now been at Aberdeen for just over two months and were completely settled in. One afternoon Benny rushed into the hut flushed with excitement. 'Come and look at this', he cried. We followed him across the square filled with curiosity, for it took a lot to excite Benny to this extent.

There at the camp gate stood a motley collection of matelots wearing an odd assortment of army shorts, civvy trousers, the occasional naval cap, but no kitbags or cases, just the jumble of clothes they stood up in. They were barely recognisable as the bunch of jubilant telegraphists that had cheered us on our way at Chatham, giving us the two finger salute (for victory of course) as we were drafted off to Africa in their place. We laughed till the tears rolled down our faces as they poured their story out to the only audience in the world who wouldn't have lent a sympathetic ear. Apparently they were aboard a converted liner having a whale of a time, half the men aboard were three parts drunk on the cheap beer as the ship sailed towards Gibraltar at a steady twenty knots. She was alone because she was too fast for the average convoy and not an easy target for a sub unless she sailed right across her bows.

Unfortunately she wasn't as fast as the Focke Wolf Condor which came literally out of the blue and straddled her with a stick of bombs. There were more casualties than needs be as drunks don't react quickly enough to an emergency and that was the last time that troopships sold beer to the troops. However, all our mates survived and it seemed the only thing that got hurt was their pride.

They were picked up by a destroyer and dumped at Freetown like a bunch of refugees. I marvelled that once again I had missed the action simply because of a clerical error. You obviously have to work at it to become a hero.

Carpenter Again

They completed their joining routine and were kitted out and we bought them their beer in the mess that night for they had no money, then they asked us what the action was like in Aberdeen, which was also the unlikely name of the village the other side of the mangrove swamp, hence we were HMS Aberdeen.

We assured them that nothing ever happened in this neck of the woods and the following day just to prove us liars my old pal the carpenter went berserk. He was high on 'Red Biddy' or methylated spirits if you prefer, and ran round and round the camp waving a machete round his head. The CO came out of his quarters and with an immediate grasp of the situation bellowed, 'Stop that man!' which of course would have immediately solved the problem, but it reminded me of the story of the mouse who told the others that if they tied a bell round the cat's neck they would know when he was coming, but another mouse asked, 'But who is going to tie the bell on?'

Clearly none of us fancied tying a bell round a mad, machete-wielding carpenter's neck, indeed some were rebellious enough to suggest to the CO that he must be bloody joking as we all stood well back, while the carpenter cleared the main square.

Eventually the Chief drew a revolver from the armoury and sent a shot whistling over the chippy's head. It seemed to sober him up far quicker than black coffee ever could and, quick as a flash, he disappeared into the mangrove swamp and never returned, which considering he was good for ninety days in the brig wasn't surprising.

Anyone for Swimming?

The good thing about our camp site was that we were only five minutes' walk from Lumley beach which was a magnificent stretch of sand and in those days was miles from anywhere. Although a lot of the lads used to sunbathe in the nude, I noticed that they all put their trunks on when they went for a swim.

There had to be a reason for this, so I asked an old hand why they were all overcome by modesty on entering the water? He was only too happy to enlighten me. 'Don't go out too far or the sharks will get you, and don't swim in the raw because the barracudas rip off anything that's dangling, if you see what I mean. Your trunks also protect your vitals from the Portuguese Man of War which is about the worst kind of jelly fish you can get. Its sting leaves weals all over your body and it's really painful, so the last thing you want is to get its tentacles round your testicles. Enjoy your swim!'

Believe it or not I've read a holiday brochure recently that advertised a luxury hotel on Lumley Beach with wonderful swimming in tropical waters. They probably sell them a one-way ticket!

The Soft Green Couch

'Gus-Gus' admitted he couldn't swim, which took us completely by surprise, but he confidently predicted he would be swimming in a week or two. 'It's just a case of mind over matter', he said firmly. We should have known better than to take the remark lightly from Mr 200%.

He bided his time and on the day when the sea was as rough as I've ever seen it, he flung himself in and struck out for the horizon. In no time at all he was wallowing in the waves and began disappearing beneath them. It took three of our strongest swimmers, aided by the rest of us forming a chain, to get him out. We pumped him out on the beach and then rushed him to Freetown General Hospital.

The following day I went along with Benny and Bugsie

to visit him. 'How do you feel, Gus?' we asked. Gus was right back to his old self. 'Smashing', he replied, 'it was like lying on a soft green couch, and I heard music. I shall never be afraid of drowning again!'

The incident reached the CO's ears and he instructed Gus to only go into the sea when Leading Telegraphist Mackintosh (who was his killick of the hut and a particularly good swimmer) was with him. And to Mac he added, 'If you want to get him off your back, I suggest you teach him to swim.' It was a recipe for success for Gus-Gus was mad keen to learn and Mac was just as keen to get shot of him, and in no time at all Gus was splashing about with the rest of us.

Winter Woes

At long last we had encouraging reports that the German army's relentless march across the face of the world had run into trouble. True to form they had swept across Russia just as they had done to the rest of Europe, but Hitler had overlooked two important factors. One was the incredibly bitter Russian winters, and the second was the enormous distance across Russia.

Consequently by the end of 1942 he had reached Stalingrad with an exhausted over-extended army, which was met by an unbelievably hostile and bitter opposition. The Russians had burnt everything for hundreds of miles as the Germans advanced, and they were now fighting for every street and every house as the frozen enemy tried to wrest Stalingrad from their grip.

It was all too much for the Germans. Their supply lines were stretched for an immense distance across frozen wastes and those that weren't killed by the Russians were suffering beyond belief as the Russian winter took its toll. It was a far cry from those halcyon days when they were storming across Europe with the sun on their backs and their panzers crushing all before them.

Rommel Still Tops

By January 1943 the Germans inside Stalingrad surrendered in their thousands and gave Adolf his first major setback of the war. From then on the dread of every man in the Wehrmacht was to be sent to the Eastern Front.

However in North Africa Rommel was still being difficult and gave the Americans their first taste of war against the Africa Korps by decisively beating them in the battle of Kasserine Pass in Tunisia.

He was still in my top ten list of heroes. Why couldn't the man have been a Brit?

The Laundry Lesson

We each employed a dhobi boy at the 'exhorbitant' rate of six shillings a month, plus all the soap he needed. As we wore all white during the day and white long sleeved shirts at dusk for night clothing to keep the mosquitos at bay, this didn't seem over-generous and at the end of the month I gave my boy (who was considerably older than I was) a packet of twenty cigarettes for good measure. I was gently rebuked in the mess that night by Angus, a fierce-looking Scot with a red beard. 'Y're making a mistake, laddie, it doesn't work like that out here. They only respect you if you're firm and act superior. If you treat them like brothers, they think you're soft and take liberties'. I didn't have long to wait to find that he 'spake sooth'. My very next bundle of dhobi came back minus my best shirt.

'Somebody tef 'em', my boy said, and I was stymied.

He was adamant that he had hung it on the line and it had gone when he came back for it. My instinct for fair play made me give him the benefit of the doubt for I had no proof whatsoever to the contrary. That night in the mess I consulted the oracle with the red beard and he doubled up with laughing. 'The only thief that pinched your shirt was your own boy "Sammy la Conte", but it's no problem. Just take him on one side and lean on him and if he hasn't already flogged it, he'll bring it back.'

Next day I took Sammy behind the hut and cuffed him round the ear in between demands for my shirt to be returned. It took four good cuffs and I was beginning to get worried that I was committing an injustice before he finally broke.

'I think I might know someone who has it, boss', he croaked. 'I try to get it off him tomorrow'. True to the oracle's prediction, my shirt was duly returned, immaculately pressed and we agreed now that we had an understanding that that would be the end of the matter. I was never over-generous with my cigarettes again. I limited it to two or three fags if there was more dhobi than usual, and Sammy seemed quite content with that.

Tot Time

We had settled down to a routine of watchkeeping and there was always someone asleep in our hut until at least noon when they piped 'up spirits' and the ship became alive when we queued up for our rum ration. As the alternative to taking your tot was threepence a day almost everyone took their tot and swapped it with non-smokers like me for their tobacco ration (known as tickler) if they couldn't get on with it, for rum is very much an acquired taste.

I used to savour my second tot for when I came off watch, it was as good as any sleeping pill, just before you slipped into your bunk.

Much later I rose to the exalted rank of 'rum bosun' which was a pretty demanding role. I would receive the rations for eighty hands from the duty officer and stand by the barrel with the measure and fill their motley receptacles, such as filed down halves of beer bottles or enamel mugs or even a soap dish, for the only real glasses were in the wardroom.

If they were reasonably friendly towards you (and most of them were) they would say the magic word 'sippers' and you would take the merest sip from the measure before pouring it in. All the gash in the bottom of the barrel was the responsibility of the rum bosun and must be poured away. Not surprisingly I poured it away down the throats of myself and two or three 'oppos' which on top of fifty or sixty 'sippers' made me feel good and ready to take on the entire German navy but unfortunately Admiral Donetz's fleet didn't get involved with mangrove swamps in Sierra Leone.

'Crack of Doom'

Yet another batch of Special Operators arrived, only half a dozen this time, and the Londoners among us soon began to wish that the clerk at Chatham had run true to form and inadvertantly sent them to Outer Mongolia. Among them was a lugubrious character with a seemingly never-ending string of tales of woe concerning the terrible time they were having in the capital. His name was Jack Boom and in no time at all he was known as 'Crack of Doom', but unfortunately there was a lot of truth in the tales he told and it didn't do much for our morale.

We knew that the really big raids had stopped as long ago as May 1941 and anything after that was merely a nuisance, but 'crack of doom' wasn't going to let us off that easily. He was very well informed about the new hit and run raiders which were twin engined bombers (mostly Messerschmitt 110s) which came in low under the radar screen, dropped their bombs and scuttled off home even before the barrage balloons could be raised or the alarm sounded.

They had hit a school at Lewisham killing many children and they caused a terrible disaster at Bethnal Green underground station when their arrival out of the blue caused a mad rush for the shelter and a woman and her baby fell down the stairs causing a domino effect. With people still trying to get in the result was horrendous and 178 people were either crushed to death or died of suffocation in the resultant pile-up.

Death at the Palais

I have condensed the story into a few lines, but Jack Boom could make it last for half an hour, savouring each detail. For the West Londoners he had especially juicy tale of a bomb landing on Hammersmith Palais when the dancing was at its height, killing over 300 dancers and any of the lads whose girlfriends were regulars at the Palais (and there were several) could cheerfully have throttled 'crack of doom'.

It was a great pity that Boom had come to us from London with his tales instead of North Africa where the news was considerably brighter and at last we'd got the Germans on the run. By the end of June 1943 they were finally mopped up and Monty was looking at the next stepping stone — Sicily!

The Biggest Battle

In July the biggest battle of all time was taking place at the Kursk Salient, but if you had stopped any Cockney in the street and asked him where it was, you'd have drawn a complete blank. 'We've got enough problems 'ere wot with rationing and the ruddy bombs, mate!'

In fact it was north of Kharkov in Russia (or the Ukraine to be more precise), and was the most savage and bitter and by far the biggest German attack of the whole war. The Russians repelled them and inflicted enormous casualites on the Germans, and by the middle of July the great German retreat began and it was the beginning of the end for Hitler, although he was to give his people two more years of suffering and torment before they could finally lay down their arms.

If only 'crack of doom' could have told us about these tremendous victories instead of how our friends and relatives were still living through hell, we'd have felt a whole lot better, but I have a feeling that even if he'd known about them, he wouldn't have told us — it just wasn't his style.

One thing was for sure, he wasn't on my short list for heroes.

The Night Watchman

The middle watch came off at 4 a.m. and most of them slept in until 11 a.m. or so, if they were not disturbed, but the best laid plans of mice and men. . . From out of the blue we acquired a moslem night watchman who moreover was a very devout gentleman, so what could be more natural than at the crack of dawn he should spread his mat at the back of our hut, face towards Mecca and start catawailing at the top of his voice.

He was unlucky that Benny (he of the huge frame and the short fuse) had the bunk nearest the door and received the full blast of his entreaties to Allah right in his ear, just as he was dreaming no doubt of being molested by twenty beautiful maidens.

'What the bloody hell's going on?' he demanded and pausing only to put his boots on and nothing else, he dashed out of the hut to be confronted by our devout friend with his forehead touching the ground and his rear pointing to the sky, pouring his heart out at a million decibels.

The inevitable happened, the night watchman was unceremoniously dispatched by Benny and ran off still shouting at a million decibels, but this time the words seemed rather different.

Gus's Mystery Parcel

Gus-Gus had been quiet for too long and our suspicions were aroused when a well-wrapped parcel, obviously containing an oblong box arrived, which Gus collected with great joy and invited us to witness the opening ceremony.

'Bottles of rum?' we asked hopefully. Gus shook his head. 'Some decent food at last?' Another 'no'. 'Well, what else is worth sending a couple of thousand miles?' we demanded.

Triumphantly he unwrapped the package and withdrew — horror of horrors — a violin! Not that I'm averse to a violin if it's played by Stephan wots-his-name, or even Yehudi Menuhin, but without even hearing a note we just knew what Gus would sound like. Our worse fears were soon confirmed as he scraped that wretched bow to and fro until it fairly set your teeth on edge and Benny summed up our mutual feelings with a terse 'Shit in it, Gus', which is the naval equivalent of 'Will you kindly desist'. But Mr 200% had found a new skill to master and as he ferociously scraped away he earnestly explained, 'I am not going to let this thing beat me'.

For four or five days he made our lives a nightmare. You couldn't come into the hut without finding him on the edge of his bunk scraping away like fury and we began to rebel.

Music Hath Charms

Realising he was pushing his luck, Gus went across the square and squatted with an unsuspecting friend. The occupants of the hut stuck it for nearly an hour, which was longer than I thought they would and then Gus was forcibly evicted. Indeed, they were so incensed that they stuck a notice on the door which said, 'Dogs, wogs and Gus keep out!'

Never one to give in, Gus was back the next day with his instrument of torture and seeing the hut was empty, he plunged into an orgy of scraping and wailing. What he didn't realise was that Benny (yes, he of the short fuse again) had come off the morning watch and was blissfully snoozing under his mosquito net. With a howl of fury, Benny leapt from his bunk and wrenching the offending 'Strad' from Gus's arms, he fetched it an almighty blow across his shoulders and the instrument disintegrated in a shower of strings and plywood.

Gus was inconsolable, but Benny was completely unmoved and went straight back to his bunk and was asleep in two minutes flat, just as though he'd got up to put the cat out. Which I suppose isn't a bad comparison.

That evening we took Gus into the canteen and bought his beer, and even Benny chipped in, although secretly most of us thought we should be buying a beer for Benny as well.

Snatchback

March 1943 had been the worst month of the war for Allied shipping in the Atlantic as we operators at HMS Aberdeen were well aware by the frenzied activity on the air as the U-boats called their packs to home-in on convoy after convoy, and I ground my teeth in frustration as we took bearings on them while ship after ship went to Davey Jones Locker.

So I was pleasantly surprised when at the beginning of August the skipper passed on the welcome news that we hadn't lost an Allied ship in the Atlantic since the middle of May, and the Special Operators had played a major part in this success. The U-boat packs had been split up and were licking their wounds and had become thoroughly demoralised.

What the CO didn't stress (or probably didn't know) was that a large part of this success was due to a new radar being fitted to Coastal Command aircraft which enabled them to detect the U-boats in rough seas or at night when they had to surface to recharge their batteries, but Admiral Doenitz made the point forcibly to Hitler that he had lost nearly a third of his submarines at sea in one month and it couldn't go on. However, it was good for our morale to believe it was all down to the Royal Navy and with hindsight, I gave the skipper ten out of ten. I winced when someone suggested we deserved a special medal — in the modern idiom it would have been represented by a couch potato.

As a titbit he added that Mussolini had been imprisoned by the Italians and Marshal Badaglio had been made P.M. If he had hung on until September 12th before he told us, he could have added that in an audacious rescue the German Paras had snatched Mussolini back again, but like all bad news in wartime it was played down and we had captured Cassino monastery (or rather the Poles had) before I heard that he was back in circulation.

The Ferry

There was a ferry which plied from the native village across the mangrove swamps and picked up the main road to Freetown, saving about a ten miles detour along the beach to Lumley and back. It was a pretty primitive affair and we only used it for fun as we could always get a lift into town in the supply lorry if we needed it. I was waiting at the landing stage with a chap from my old class at Brighton, who had the reputation of being the ship's sex maniac. He certainly was keen but even he had to curb his habits in Sierra Leone. The risks were pretty high and they tell of one whore in Freetown who put the entire ship's company of a corvette out of action by passing on her good wishes and everything else.

It was probably a slight exaggeration, for these stories grow with the telling, but certainly VD was rife around this neck of the woods and there was a nasty rumour (probably scurrilous) that Lady Astor had suggested that all troops returning from Freetown should wear a yellow armband to warn the girls at home that we were a bad bet.

The natives seemed to inherit gonorrhoea as a way of life and treated it with the same regard as we did a common cold. I was reminded how Captain Cook and his merry men sailed among the unsuspecting Polynesians who welcomed them with open arms and other parts of their anatomy and discovered that the first benefits of Western civilization was a hefty dose of the clap, which unlike the cheap baubles and beads, will stay with them for eternity.

The More Things Change. ..

It seemed highly possible that Freetown which had been a major port since the days of the slave trade, when large numbers of liberated slaves were deposited there from 1787 onward, had also reaped the same dubious benefit from generations of seamen. It became a major problem among the native naval ratings, not so much with the labour force but definitely among the lads who helped the cook in the galley.

The MO called on his routine inspection and found that eight of the twelve lads working in the galley had gonorrhoea. He was a fairly recent arrival in Africa and he got in a rare flap and rushed over to the CO pointing out that these lads were handling food and must be replaced.

The CO obligingly ordered a big reshuffle and those with the pox were found jobs outside. A month later the MO returned and inspected the galley staff and discovered that eight out of the twelve had VD!

The Chief said it was just maintaining the 'Status quo'.

Small Small

Meanwhile back at the landing stage my present companion was passing the time winding up a youth of about fifteen years of age by pointing to the huge bulge at the front of his shorts.

'Small, small', he said, grinning at the indignant youth.

Now some of the natives might be small in some parts of their anatomy but in that department they rarely are and, as he had intended he had hurt the lad's pride. An indignant denial was followed by his tormentor's next barb. 'You picken (child) you small small'. It didn't take long before the youth had undone his flies and was producing the evidence before a small crowd, none of whom batted an eyelid, that he was anything but 'small small'.

Now with a sly grin my mate said, 'You picken, it doesn't work'. More heated denials and then came the final twist of the knife. 'It doesn't work, you pull yourself to prove it. If it works, I dash you one fag'. In no time at all the lad was masturbating in front of a curious audience which had grown by now to some forty or fifty people.

It took a little longer than expected, possibly he found the public performance off-putting, and by the time he had finished half his audience had embarked on the ferry which had arrived from across the swamp. No one said a word until one old lady could contain herself no longer.

'You fool to pull yourself for one fag', she said, 'You should have got twenty!' And with a snort of contempt she wheeled round and joined the queue.

The Witch Doctor

The village itself had only just been jerked into the twentieth century by the war. The entire population would stand in the stream which ran parallel with the main street at a convenient two hundred yards distance, all without a stitch on and soap themselves down and pour water over each other, all the time laughing happily together so naturally that I couldn't help feeling it was a shame we had to come along and spoil it.

They had a secret society that used to meet at night in a hut hidden by reed woven fences and none of the villagers would go within a mile of the place when the elders were in a session. I suspected some sort of voodoo, for I can't think of anything else that would induce such terror into the locals.

I met the local witch doctor once (in broad daylight I hasten to add) and he certainly was a cut above the ordinary. The villagers held him in awe and not surprisingly so, for he was well worth becoming a member of the magic circle. Among his repertoire was the ability to push a six inch nail — and I mean a real one — completely up his right nostril! I was impressed for he was also very articulate. Not that he spoke impeccable English, far from it, but his pigeon-English was littered with proverbs and shrewd observations which he didn't get from Shakespeare or Confucious as he'd spent the past sixty years in the African bush.

Capsize

Soon a terrible tragedy was to befall the village. The monsoons broke and the ferry which was halfway across the swamp was caught by a huge gust of wind and overturned. Thirty-five people were drowned which was about 10% of the population, and the natives were devastated. For three days and nights the drums rolled and the weeping and wailing could be heard for miles. Indeed, in our camp we seemed to be right in the middle of it as the lamentations drifted across the swamp, and by the third day it was really getting to us. Fortunately it did not affect our watch on the U-boats as we wore earphones and could turn the volume up on our radios, which was just as well for if the CO had been forced to send the Chief down to tell them to shut up, we would well have had an international incident on our hands.

They had a mass funeral which was a really magnificent occasion, but none of our lads went to watch — it didn't seem right to intrude on their private grief.

However, I did see a couple of funerals at a later date and the contrast in styles was amazing. In the first there was a crowd of mourners following the hearse, beating their breasts and wailing piteously. I found out later that most of them were hired to make the numbers up.

In the second the hearse was followed by a leaping, happy throng who were obviously having a ball. I turned to my local friend and asked about the palpable difference between the two. 'Ah', he said, 'the first funeral was that of a child who was taken from us too soon and everyone is sad. The second was an old man who had lived a full and happy life and everyone is glad for him'.

I had to admit there was a certain amount of logic in their thinking.

Worried

By now I was getting seriusly worried about the progress of the war. The invasion of Sicily had gone well and we were poised on the springboard to leap into Italy which we could reasonably claim was the second front which the Russians had been demanding for over a year.

Not that I blamed Winston for withholding his hand. The Reds weren't on our side from choice, indeed in 1940 when we stood alone, if they could have shared Great Britain with Germany as they had done to Poland, they wouldn't have hesitated, so why not let the two former allies slug it out to the death?

So why was I getting worried about the progress of

the war? I hear you asking. Because it was all going far too well and time was running out for 'yours truly'. I could safely reckon on another year in this dump and my chances of even seeing a German, let alone becoming a hero were rapidly diminishing.

The Yanks in the Pacific were beginning to dig in at long last and stem the yellow tide, a fact which Tokyo Rose studiously ignored, but she did give the Yanks at Rainbow corner at Piccadilly a mention.

'The Americans have invented a new kind of fibre called nylon and are making the most beautiful stockings with it. The only people who have them at the moment are the GIs, so if your wife or girl friend is wearing them, she's been hanging around Rainbow Corner!'

Of course it wasn't strictly accurate, but there was enough of the half-truth in the message to twist the knife. What a war!

The POWs

However, even as I brooded a large number of the opposition were landing at Freetown, but alas dear reader, it was nowhere near as exciting as it sounds. The enemy landing consisted of several thousand Italian POWs who had been rounded up in North Africa from Tripoli to Abyssinia and dumped out of harm's way in Sierra Leone.

It was a shrewd move for they were put into camps with barbed wire round them and virtually no guards to speak of, for there was absolutely nowhere for them to go. Not that most of them wanted to go anywhere anyway, they had had quite enough of Mussolini and his war, thank you very much, and a more broken, dispirited bunch I've never seen.

Before long the authorities let them out for a few hours to wander round the town in small groups, but if they got in our way we would just sweep them off the pavement and they took it without a murmur — not that they had much choice. They were probably counting their blessings that they hadn't been captured by the Russians on the Eastern Front.

The Artists

To this day I am still amazed that the Italians, who must be the world's worst soldiers, can spawn a sinister mob like the Mafia who with a mere handful of men, can terrorise and put a stranglehold on such a powerful nation as the USA. But while they may not be the bravest nation in the world, they are certainly one of the world's most artistic people.

The word soon got around that the POWs were making all sorts of beautiful things out of any material they could get their hands on, and on our next day off Bugsie and I went to see for ourselves. We walked straight into the camp which now had no guards at all, just a couple of administrators, and after a brief tour of inspection which was rather like walking round a high-class arts and crafts exhibition, I ordered a cigarette case for my father, ornately carved with a beautiful design and inscribed with his initials and Sierra Leone 1943. I considered it a pound well spent, and this wonderful piece of memorabilia is still in my family's possession to this day.

The maker of this object d'art confided to me that he had already spent over ten years in Africa, starting as a young soldier in Italian Somaliland in 1933 when he had been in the forefront of Marshal Graziani's invasion force when Mussolini violated Abyssinia in 1935 and had spent most of that time looking over his shoulder for the next spear or bullet, and he was heartily sick of the place.

'Well at least you can stop looking over your shoulder', I replied, and clutching my work of art I went back to Aberdeen to listen to those elusive U-boats, tanterlisingly beyond my reach.

Dispatch Riders

The CO was now beginning to build his little empire around him, just like any ambitious civil servant at home. The more buildings and men he surrounded himself with, the more quickly he would become a two and a half ringer, so one of the little ploys he came up with was to employ a naval dispatch rider to take important messages to the main RN Barracks at Kissi, just outside Freetown. In the first instance he would use one of us and then when the job was firmly established, he would apply for a regular D.R.

He called for three volunteers with motor bike experience and on the principle that a change is as good as a holiday, I stepped forward, promptly followed by a tall, thin Londoner called 'Toddy', and the third volunteer was the inevitable Gus-Gus.

The Chief gathered us round him and explained the bike was over by the guard house and that we were to familiarise ourselves with it today and we'd be ready to start operations tomorrow. I was thrilled but slightly apprehensive and as we gathered round the ancient Norton I confessed to the other two that I hadn't actually ridden a motor bike before, so I hoped they would show me the ropes. At this Toddy confessed that he hadn't ridden one either, but he had thought the same as I did that he'd pick it up off the other two.

We both looked expectantly at Gus who didn't seem at all perturbed by the situation and wore the air of an expert.

'Well,' he said, 'I've never actually ridden one, but there can't be much to it, I've seen quite young kids at home belting about on them.' Toddy rolled his eyes at me but by now Mr 200% was in full cry. He was astride the bike, flicked the petrol switch on and began kicking merrily away at the starter. The good old reliable Norton burst into life and awaited instructions from its new master.

'A Piece of Cake'

Gus was jubiliant. 'See, it's a piece of cake', he cried as he revved up like mad and then with a whoop he put it into gear and hurtled forward like a Grand Prix start except that he was jumping and leaping into the air like a bucking bronco. He disappeared from sight in a cloud of smoke and dust, leaving Toddy and me open-mouthed.

For a full minute we listened to the roar of the receding Norton, then there was a dull thud and then silence. We looked around helplessly, wondering what to do when through the camp gate came the supply lorry, just at the right time. We flagged him down and clambered aboard explaining our predicament to the driver and in just about twice the time it had taken Gus, we reached the crossroads where all was revealed.

'Write-Off'

There was the local bus with a bit of a dent in its side, but otherwise unharmed with a sea of black faces peering out of the windows, and there was Gus sitting at the roadside nursing what turned out to be a broken arm.

It was a small miracle that that was all that was wrong with him for the bike had carried on after he had fallen off and wrapped itself round a tree, and was as near a write-off as made no odds.

We walked back to camp to explain it in as delicate a manner as possible to the Chief that in fifteen minutes from the time he had given us the 'off', Gus had written the bike off. It was just as well that he was already back in the General Hospital because if he'd come back with us the Chief would have put him in there anyway.

The next day we went to visit him and he was sitting up and looking quite perky and completely unabashed. 'That bloody fool bus driver', he snorted, 'he ought to know he should give way to a naval vehicle'. And then indignantly, 'And he must have seen I didn't know how to stop the thing. I wonder if the CO will get us another bike?'

Toddy rolled his eyes to heaven and said, 'Gus, don't you sometimes think that it might be you that's out of step with the rest of the world, instead of the other way round?'

Dhobi Problem

I was suddenly faced with a domestic problem. Sammy, my dhobi boy, was transferring to the main naval barracks at Kissi and as I could not find a suitable replacement, I decided to have a crack at it myself. I found it hard work and very time consuming, but at least the laundry dried pretty quickly in the tropical sun and I felt quite smug as I hung out my first wash on a long line at the back of the heads.

I had nearly reached my hut and was idly listening

to a workman who was rethatching our roof, calling to another workman who was walking towards the heads carrying a soggy bundle of reeds. He strode past my washing and as he drew level he half-turned, looking back at the man on the roof and still walking, dragged the end of the bundle the whole length of my line of dhobi, leaving a filthy black trail on each item. I sprinted over to him and arrived just as he put the bundle on the ground to continue the conversation. The tempting target was absolutely irrisistable, and I gave it a hefty boot which propelled him face-first into his mucky bundle.

He stood up wiping the muck from his face, absolutely livid with rage and equally livid, I pointed to my washing. He weighted up his chances of putting me in hospital, thought better of it and strode off.

Defaulters

What I didn't know was that he strode straight round to the Chief and made a complaint that I'd assaulted him, with the result that I was lined up in defaulters next morning. The workman told his version to the CO and then I told mine. When I got to the bit where he bent over just as he'd finished laying a trail of muck along the length of my dhobi, the CO's lips twitched at the corner and I could see his imagination working overtime and the case was dismissed with a stern warning to exercise more self-control in future, or there would be dire consequences.

Outside I gave a cocky smirk to my accuser and went back to the gang to tell them that all's right with the world.

The Fall Guy

My victory was short-lived, however, for my African brothers were already plotting my downfall, and completely unsuspecting I took the bait. It was nearly a week later when I was in charge of the supply lorry to draw stores from Kissi and I had two workmen to assist me (who I now realise were mates of my antagonist of the week previous) and a coloured naval driver.

We drew the stores without incident and were half-way back to camp when one of the workmen appeared to lose his balance and knocked a heavy box off the pile beside him, and it hit me on the leg. It wasn't too painful but I swore at him almost as a matter of course. He immediately tripped over the next box and fell heavily and with hindsight, deliberately upon me, thumping me on the arm as he landed.

Enough was enough and I pushed him roughly away, whereupon he did an impersonation of 'Maradonna' when he's tackled in the penalty area, and shot over backwards across the nearest pile of boxes and lay there screaming and waving his legs in the air. The driver looked back through the window and seeing what looked like a serious accident braked as hard as he could, sending boxes everywhere.

By the time he got round to the back of the lorry the other two were screaming accusations at me that I'd assaulted a man just because he fell against me when the lorry swerved, and they could hardly wait to get back to lay a charge against me.

The High Jump

Next morning I was back on defaulters again and this time I knew I was for the high jump. In vain I protested that I'd been set up but I had to admit I barely knew the two workmen and when the driver (whom I am sure was not in on the plot) gave his version of the incident, how he looked through his window and saw the 'victim' lying on his back among a pile of boxes, screaming his head off, I was sunk without a trace.

I knew the CO this time had to be seen to be fair in the eyes of the blacks, and I was given seven days number elevens, which could have been a lot worse and indicated to me that he half thought it might have been a set-up.

Nevertheless three or four hours extra chores and drill can be pretty demanding in between watchkeeping and the workmen were waiting outside with even cockier grins than I wore last week. We all knew they'd got the result they were after.

Number Elevens

The number eleven's squad was rather larger than usual because the defaulters had been expanded by another half-a-dozen who had been involved in a punch-up in the liberty lorry on its way back from Freetown.

There was a tremendous rumpus and the Chief had to stop the lorry and come round the back and sort it out, with the result that they were all put on a charge. I could have told the CO without seeing the incident who was responsible.

The main culprits were a Geordie and a Scot who were inseparable 'Oppos' and were great company until they'd had a few drinks and then they turned into monsters. They would go berserk on the slightest provocation and smash up bars, restaurants, police stations — you name it.

On this occasion they were well gone and a chance

remark was siezed upon and the balloon went up. I'd bet my last dime that the other four were merely protecting themselves, but it sounds a likely story to tell the CO.

Hence there were seven of us that bright, sunny morning all parading in our working gear as per instructions and wondering what delights the Chief had in store for us.

Whitewash

'You're going to work for your living this morning', he leered, 'you're going to whitewash the mess roof and you don't come down till it's finished. If you pull your fingers out, you'll have time for a meal and a shower before you go on watch'. He motioned towards a pile of brushes and paint cans and shouted, 'Now get cracking!' We dutifully shinned up the ladders wearing only slippers and shorts, for we were used to the sun by now, and 'got cracking'.

After an hour so so we were still painting like fury, when 'Scouse' who not surprisingly came from Liverpool, gave an over zealous motion with his brush and flicked a modicum of paint over Harry, a lad from Cornwall with an accent you could cut with a knife. Harry gave out the Cornish equivalent of 'watch it' and promptly flicked a brushful back at Scouse. Unfortunately his aim wasn't all that good and I caught more of it than Scouse.

Play the White Man

Entering into the spirit of the thing, I collected a whole brushful and gave Harry the lot. At least I meant to give

Harry the lot, but half of it went over 'Geordie' who was mostly responsible for us having a quorum in sufficient numbers to warrent being on the roof in the first place. We held our breath — we needed another punch-up like a hole in the head — but at that time of the day Geordie was completely sober and was wearing his Mr Nice Guy hat.

With a grin he flicked a brushful back at me and for good measure another brushful at 'Pickles' a Londoner with a great sense of humour and a very peaceful disposition, who if he'd been born twenty years later would have ended up in San Francisco recommending 'Flower Power' to the world. Just like a chain letter, Pickles dutifully passed the paint on with the obligatory two extra copies, and in the flicker of an eyelid, everyone on the roof was flicking whitewash at everyone else and a small crowd began to gather below and were soon joined by the duty officer and the Chief.

By this time we had abandoned flicking and were standing toe to toe and painting each other from head to foot. The crowd looked apprehensively at the duty officer and the Chief who was poised to run amok at the nod of the officer's head. There was a pregnant pause and then from nowhere the sub-lieutenant produced a camera and began snapping away, laughing his head off at the same time. Then with a nod he said, 'Carry on, Chief', and disappeared in the direction of the Ward Room.

Barrack Room Lawyer

The Chief, somewhat disappointed by his reaction, settled for a display of his vocal chords. 'All right, you 'orrible lot, back to work and if there's any more messing about, I'll have your guts for garters'.

We resumed our chores and finished in good time for a shower and our 'chop' which the galley boys called our meals, but be sure your sins will find you out, it took us about an hour to scrub the whitewash off and we were rather sore at the end of it. Thank goodness we kept our shorts on.

The Chief and I had always had an uneasy relationship. He regarded me as the barrack room lawyer, which I must admit was very near the truth as I'd always got an opinion and advice for the rest of the lower deck (not necessarily always the best advice, but always positive) and he disliked all H.O. (Hostilities Only) Ratings on principle. Personally I thought he was as thick as two planks of wood and as unimaginative as any CPO who had served fifteen years as a regular. I often wondered what he'd do when his twenty-one years service was up — always assuming the war had ended.

The Extra Watch

He proudly proclaimed on one occasion that he'd had sex with nineteen different nationalities, which considering he'd probably paid for most of them, hardly seemed to qualify for an Order of Merit.

However, at this point in time, the ball was firmly in my court. The Chief had 'got me over a barrel' for seven days and he was going to make the most of it. Between drills he threw every crummy job that was going at me and it was with some surprise that I heard him say that I had been excused punishment the next day. I had been around too long to expect something for nothing and I waited for the punch line and sure enough it came. 'Instead you will go with Williams on the relief lorry and share the evening watch with him'.

I should explain that down at Lumley We had a

direction finding hut and one of our men sat there every watch and took a bearing on every U-boat we heard in the main hut. The controller simply tapped out the frequency it was on and the man at Lumley then plugged into one of his sets already tuned in to that channel and took a bearing, all within five seconds of the Jerry tapping his key. Our two D.F. posts were five miles apart so if they both got the U-boat it gave us a reasonable idea of its position.

The Volunteer

Before I had recovered from the rosy spectacle of sitting in the cosy hut with Williams sharing mugs of coffee, the Chief broke in on my reverie with a further explanation. 'As you probably know, someone's been giving our Lumley operators a hard time when it gets dark. They prowl round the hut beating tom-toms and banging on the shutters and generally putting the fear of the Lord up our operator who can't leave his post if he wanted to — and I suspect not all that many of them want to know anyway, so we need a volunteeer to sort it out and you've just volunteered. So don't think you're going to sit in that hut all night drinking mugs of coffee with Williams (this was my first experience of mental telepathy), you are going to hide in a ditch and observe and if you think you can do anything you may use your initiative (followed by a contemptuous snort) but make sure nothing interferes with our work! I think more than one observer would be too obvious and they wouldn't show, so go and draw a bayonet from the armoury — just to protect yourself and don't look for any help from me if you make a mess of it.'

Well it wasn't quite like taking on the Boche, but you had to start somewhere and this was as near an enemy as I was likely to find for a thousand miles or so (Italian POWs excepted).

So tingling with excitement and great expectation I boarded the lorry bound for the evening watch at Lumley — well it certainly beat drilling in the noonday sun or whitewashing stones outside the Ward Room.

A hundred yards from the hut the lorry slowed down and I hopped over the tail board and disappeared into the bush, wearing my black trousers, black boots and black jersey — Home Fleet issue — and clutching my trusty bayonet I crawled into a dry ditch some twenty-five yards from the hut where I was well hidden under the shadow of a small bush and yet could clearly see anything that approached the hut. Davey Crocket, eat your heart out!

Voodoo

After an hour or so had dragged by I was getting pretty bored but I passed the time turning the situation over in my mind. The only reason I was here was because I'd been set up by a pair of 'baskets' in that supply lorry. Wouldn't it be great if they showed up, but it was more likely to be that voodoo mob in the village that were responsible, but then again they could be anybody. They didn't go around wearing badges.

It was almost ten o'clock when I heard the first sound, faint at first but then quite definitely and then shadowy figures appeared in indian file and began circling the hut to the steady beat of the tom-tom. It was a bright moonlit night but it was impossible to recognise any-one. I had difficulty telling them apart in daylight, let alone at night. They were not yet doing any damage but I guessed it must be pretty eerie inside the hut when you're alone.

They were completely engrossed in their dance and I was able to creep within ten yards of them, then suddenly their leader began pummelling on the shutters with his fists all the while making little whooping sounds, then the rest (four or five of them) joined in with a will and the hut rocked.

Naval Patrol

Another two minutes of this and it would disintegrate, so I gave my own war whoop and rushed in taking them completely by surprise. I thrust my trusty blade into the rear of the nearest invader (they don't like it up 'em) and he gave an agonised yell and staggered off into the Bush. The rest probably thinking they had run into a naval patrol, turned tail and fled. Only the leader hesitated and raised a threatening arm, so I promptly slashed at it and gave him a cut that he will probably remember to this day whenever he sees the scar. He stumbled off, groaning and cursing in the wake of his gang.

I finally persuaded a reluctant Williams to open the door and with considerable trepidation he slid back the bolts and let me in. He poured me a cup of coffee and we swapped our versions of the story with minor embellishments each time we told it, until the middle watch arrived. The intruders didn't come back that night or indeed any other night, which made me wonder if they were just playing a game after all. I cannot imagine the IRA giving up that easily.

Back at the camp the Chief was none too happy. 'Did you have to stab 'em, you stupid sod?' he moaned. 'We could have an uprising if it gets out!' But back in the hut my mates were over the moon and I was a hero for fifteen minutes, for while I was hardly likely to end up at Buckingham Palace with the congratulations of the

King ringing in my ears, at least I'd levelled the score with the opposition.

He No Come Back

I came out of our hut next morning and almost bumped into one of the workmen who had plotted my downfall in the provisions lorry, but the one who had done a 'Maradonna' and caused all the trouble was not with him. As the two were inseparable I had to ask him where his mate was.

'He no come back, he sick' came the reply and he refused to enlarge on that statement. My heart leapt, it seemed too much of a coincidence to hope for, although anyone that could stage manage the fiasco in the lorry had all the initiative to lead a tom-tom spree on our D.F. Hut, and to this day I've cherished the dream and I won't let anyone spoil it.

Misinterpreted

Back in the real world Italy had declared war on Germany and the Allies had been locked in a desperate struggle with the Boche at Anzio, and in March 1944 the RAF dropped 3000 tons of bombs on Hamburg. I thought of fires lighting up the London sky in 1940 and felt a warm glow.

For good measure the Scharnhorst had been intercepted by Admiral Fraser in the Duke of York and Admiral Burnet commanding a force of cruisers and in an epic sea battle had been battered to a standstill and finally sunk by eleven torpedoes, and now the Fleet Air Arm had severely damaged the Turpitz in her northern anchorage. Later she was sunk by the RAF at Tromso and Germany's surface fleet was no longer of any consequence.

How could all this be happening while I was stuck in a mangrove swamp waiting to be a hero?

It reminded me of a Jewish friend of mine who left Czechoslovakia in a hurry in 1938 and by 1941 found himself in the army. Like most mid-Europeans he spoke more than one lanuage — in fact he spoke five including fluent German — so with surprising insight the army made him an interpreter. True to form, however, I knew for a fact that they sent him to India.

No wonder I never got near a submarine — ours or theirs!

Meanwhile the Chief and I were eyeing each other warily every time we met. He regarded me as a cross he had to bear, only as he pointed out with his nose nearly poking my eye out, 'I'm a bloody atheist!' And for good measure he spat out, 'And as God is my witness, I shall always remember that bloody hat business'.

The Hat Business

I winced at the mention of that episode which happened about a month back.

There were five of us who had just come off the morning watch and we had twenty-four hours of freedom — but what to do with that precious time? I came up with a perfectly innocent suggestion that we all put £1 in the middle and the one who acquired the best hat as judged by a neutral committee in the canteen that night would take the kitty. The only rule was that you mustn't buy it!

The money was duly 'stuffed in' with the exception of Toddy who obliged with a promissory note until pay day and we set off with great purpose on our mission.

Bugsie and I had decided to reconnoitre the village as a likely starting point and we nonchalently strolled around trying to look as inconspicuous as two white men could in a totally black village. On our second lap of honour we saw just the thing, two elegant dandies who were probably off to meet their lady friends, one sporting a straw boater and the other a multi-coloured felt effort that was a cross between a fez and a busby. It was like manna from heaven!

We tossed for choice and having won, I chose the felt effort and Bugsy was quite happy with the straw boater.

Snatched

They came past us posing in their finery, scarcely wasting a glance in our direction and swaggered down the main street. 'Now!' I breathed to Bugsie and we about turned and silently crept up behind them and with a triumphant whoop snatched off their hats and sprinted down a side street that led straight into the bush.

Our dandies were in no condition to catch two fit young twenty-year olds and were soon trailing far behind. Once we were out of their sight we changed tack and jogged back to our camp to collapse in fits of laughter on our bunks. As we were the only two from our hut involved in the contest, our lads were already rooting for us as the likely winners.

Benny nipped out to the heads and when he returned he said, 'I don't want to worry you, but there are a couple of guys who are definitely not part of this establishment, who are fancy dressers with no hats, and they've just come through the main gate and they seem hopping mad!'

Sleeping In

I summed up the situation and realised we were due for interrogation. 'OK, you guys, if the Chief comes asking questions, you've got to swear that we've been sleeping in all morning. Meanwhile I'd better hide these ruddy hats'. I nipped off behind the heads and hid our small problem deep in the bush and returned to my bunk, adopted a somnolent posture and waited. It tok some twenty minutes while the Chief took them on a tour of the huts and when they reached ours they looked uncertainly at me and Bugsie. Both of us had beards which was their main means of identification and after some hesitation they picked us out. Unfortunately for them because fo the water shortage, half of the ship's company had grown a set including three more of the lads reclining on their bunks in our hut, otherwise positive identification would have been a mere formality.

Of course we strenuously denied it and the rest of the hut gave us an alibi and in spite of a quick search by the Chief they drew a blank and two frustrated villagers and an even more frustrated Chief retreated in a state of high dudgeon. That evening we were in the canteen with our trophies and the table covered in bottles of Black Horse beer, a Canadian beverage which certainly helped you banish any cares you may have, Chiefs, dandies and all.

We were waiting for the judges to arrive when the far door opened and the Chief strode in. I quickly passed our two hats over to Ginger behind the bar and said, 'For Christ's sake, hide these', and in a flash they disappeared from view. Two of the other contestants were not bothered as the people they had 'borrowed' their entries from hadn't even missed them yet, but I looked across at Fred and saw him swallow and turn pale in spite of his tan.

The Chief's Cap

For sheer audacity Fred should have been the winner. He'd noticed the Chief's dhobi boy cleaning a hat which obviously belonged to the great man himself, so he gave him just long enough to finish cleaning it and then went up to him and said, 'The Chief sent me over for his cap, have you finished it yet?'

He so nearly got away with it but just as the boy was going off duty he happened to pass the Chief who, by way of conversation, asked how his hat was coming along.

Explanations followed, hence the Chief striding across the canteen floor looking for Fred. Our lad put up a splendid display of injured innocence and carefully explained to the Chief that as he was there when the boy finished it, he offered to take it along for him. He felt it was the least he could do for the man who was holding the entire ship's company together. It was just unfortunate that he had got enticed into the bar just as he was on his way to make the delivery.

The Chief was on the verge of an apopletic fit, but as they say 'bullshit baffles brains' and he couldn't quite pin Fred down.

'I don't know what you bastards are up to,' he roared snatching his cap from Fred's grasp, 'but I'll get you one of these days and when I do, you'll wish you'd never been born!' Bristling with fury, he strode out of the canteen. Five minutes later the judges who had just finished the second dog watch entered 'stage right' and seated themselves round the table.

We explained how the Chief had unsportingly stolen Fred's entry and they solomnly judged the remaining four, one of which was a baseball cap and one a rather pathetic golf vizor, plus Bugsie's boater and my multi-coloured felt hat.

They decided that it was a dead heat between Bugsie and myself but felt that Fred's valient effort should not go unnoticed and finally recommended that the fiver should be stuck behind the bar and we drank it up. They further recommended that the judges should also have a beer out of it as a reward for their efforts.

A good time was had by all.

Donkey's Serenade

Next morning Bugsie and I went back to the village to make amends. We'd had our fun and the hats were of no further use to us and what's more, if the Chief ever saw them he'd have a field day.

So here we were at the back of the ramshackle bar which seemed to serve as the centre of the village high life. The only opposition was the Mission House but it seemed that there were more drunks than Christians in Aberdeen, so the bar won hands down.

At the rear of the bar two donkeys were hitched to a rail and as soon as the street was deserted we crept out of the bush and each of us produced a piece of string and deftly tied a hat on each of the donkeys who immediately started their favourite song, 'Hee Haw, Hee Haw'.

We slipped back into the bush in the nick of time for the owner's wife had come out of the bar to empty some rubbish and hearing the commotion came round the back to investigate. Her screams of merriment fetched out her husband who called out the rest of his clientele from the bar, and in no time at all a sizeable crowd had gathered round the indignant donkeys.

We crept deeper into the bush and slipped back to camp. Mission accomplished!

Soap Balls

But all this is history and right now the Chief is savouring every moment of having me under punishment. By the sixth day I had decided that enough was enough and consulting my seaman's manual as construed by yours truly, I hit upon an alternative to coming off the morning watch and parading in front of the inquisition.

I rolled two balls of yellow soap in my hand, swallowed them and went round to the sick bay 'tiffy' who was a nice boy named 'Bunny' and told him I was feeling terrible.

He took my temperature which, as per manual (sciver's version) had already begun to rise and watching my pained expression, he declared me unfit for duty and saw me back to my bunk where he tucked me in with an extra blanket.

At this point the Chief came storming into the hut looking for me and seeing me tucked up in bed, he did a passable imitation of a Red Indian war dance.

'Get out of there and on parade, you good-for-nothing layabout!' he stormed.

Whereupon Bunny with a courage I never dreamed he possessed, intervened by stepping between me and the Chief and quietly but firmly said, 'This man is sick and must not be moved'.

'Don't give me that bullshit,' roared the Chief, 'anyone can see he's sciving!'

'I have examined him and he's got a temperature', said Bunny. 'He is my patient and if you try to move him, I shall go straight to the CO'.

The Chief knew he was beaten. He would be right out of order to go against Bunny's decision and with a snarl, he turned and left the hut. His revenge would have to be put on ice. Me, I gave Bunny a grateful wave and turned over and went to sleep.

Tinia Paint

One genuine complaint I did have in common with most of the ship's company was the usual dose of skin problems. They were mostly ringworms and dhobi itch, and the cure was a liberal painting with tinia paint on the affected parts, which were predominently on the backside and the testicles.

Here Bunny was in his element and every morning he had a parade of at least a dozen men who on the command dropped their trousers and bent over while Bunny armed with a brush and assisted by a boy holding three highly-coloured pots of tinia paint, one red, one green and one purple, would move swiftly down the line painting every posterior a different colour, calling softly 'One for you, one for you', and so on.

The effect of tinia paint on your testicles was the equivalent of crouching over a camp fire with nothing on and the trick was to stand it as long as you could before you sat in a bucket of water.

Tristan da Cunha

A minor stir went round the ship with the announcement on the notice board that we were invited to apply for transfer to the new DF station that was being opened in the South Atlantic on a tiny island called Tristan da Cunha. Applicants were invited to attend a brief lecture on what was involved to be held in the canteen that evening.

Working on the principle that anything was better than this poxy mangrove swamp about three quarters of the ship's company applied, which should have told the CO something. It also made it very difficult to swap your watch so that you could attend the lecture.

Fortunately my bosom buddies, Benny and Bugsie and myself were not on duty until the middle watch, so we took a seat in the front row and waited all agog. I had a slight twinge of conscience that this would put a further two thousand miles between me and Hitler if I got the job — but I was getting no place fast in Freetown, so what the hell! We already had a DF station in the Ascencion Island with which we were in regular communication and a lieutenant from that base had set up the new station at Tristan da Cunha and had flown back to Sierra Leone to pick up his crew.

He was quite informative and told us that Tristan was the largest of a group of three islands, the other two being inaccessible (with cliffs over a thousand feet high, hence its name) and Nightingale, the smallest, barely more than one square mile in area. On almost all sides the islands are surrounded by kelp and a broad belt of this southern seaweed means a boat can approach the islands even in stormy weather. The main island where the DF station has been set up is named after a Portuguese Admiral who discovered it in 1506.

He explained that the island had changed very little since early Victorian days and that the population spoke a language that was reminiscent of the peasants in the days of Queen Anne.

High Morals Only

They were desperately poor and the inside of their houses were covered by old newspapers to keep out the draught and finally, they had a very high moral standard, so he was looking for four likely lads who would fit in with their way of life.

Surprisingly, all three of us made the short list of ten, but then I suspect the Chief put the boot in and that was the end of that. Williams made it and we gave him a grand send-off. At least he wouldn't have the voodoo warriers creeping round his hut in that remote part of the globe.

Simonstown

Shortly after this the draft chit of the entire war was up for grabs. Two men were needed at Simonstown the main South African naval base at Capetown, and without exception the entire ship's company volunteered. The tales of South African hospitality were legend throughout the fleet. Huge cars waited at the dockside to take our lads home and wine and dine them, wait on their slightest wish and their daughters were proud to go out with a British matelot (Lady Astor please note).

Their hospitality was not just confined to the navy, for any convoy that paused to refuel on its way to the Far East received a tumultous welcome and the troops who were granted two days ashore to stretch their legs (for it was a very lengthy journey round the Cape to India and all points East when you were crammed together like sardines) were flabbergasted at the warmth of their welcome, and not surprisingly one or two decided that they preferred that lifestyle to returning to that chicken coop of a troopship.

Ostracised

I felt very sad years later when we turned our backs on the South Africans who had supported us and given up the flower of their manhood through two world wars, and ostracised them without trying to understand their problems, just when they needed us to reciprocate. But then I never did understand politics and the ease with which a politician will turn his back on a friend. Once again, I digress, for meanwhile here was a chance to spend the rest of the war in paradise, with a supporting cast of big cars, grand houses and beautiful women and for that I will forfeit my Distinguished Military Cross. However, timing is all important when draft chits are being handed out and the terrible twins Jock and Geordie had got it just right. They had been involved in drunken brawls on and off for the past month and had just finished another stretch of number elevens for smashing up a table in the canteen while trying to break the cook's head with it, and the CO had had enough of their continual aggravation and couldn't get them on the ship to Simonstown fast enough. He must have felt embarrassed knowing the rest of us were mortified by the injustice of it all. Those two deserved a Murmansk convoy, not Capetown and I could visualise Britain losing that most important base in no time at all once that terrible duo arrived.

It thoroughly bore out the truth of my favourite proverb, 'Honesty pays, but not much'.

My Football Coupon

By now I was the unofficial social organiser, not because I felt an earnest desire to entertain the troops, but rather because whenever I was bored I would think up some madcap scheme to keep us amused and as the ship's bookie, there was usually an angle to make a fast buck.

For some time I'd been getting the football fixtures from the BBC and making a fixed odds coupon from the eight most difficult selections I could find. It caught on like wildfire and I even had a runner in the RAF

Air Sea Rescue Service unit on the other side of Freetown.

What they did for a living I'll never know as there were barely half a dozen planes in Sierra Leone, so they weren't exactly overworked, which was probably why they had plenty of time to study the coupon.

The Chief didn't know it but my runner in the camp provided him with a coupon, by telling him it was run by the RAF, and he dutifully filled it in and signed his name on it although gambling was strictly illegal in the navy. He even got three draws up on one occasion and I certainly begrudged paying out on that one!

In the close season I ran a book on the Derby which was once again part of the English scene and a sure sign that Germany was no longer in a position to pose a serious threat to our way of life. However, I was sticking my neck out because I hadn't a clue to the form and when I finally got a paper and read the official starting prices, it made my blood run cold, but I got away with it because the punters assumed I knew what I was doing and backed the horses I had made first and second favourites, when in actual fact they could have had ten to one about the genuine article!

The Dog Race

One set of form I did know was the three stray dogs that the lads had adopted and who were always hanging around the cookhouse. It occurred to me that with no football to bet on the lads might fancy a flutter on the dogs, and here we had the nucleus of White City Stadium on our doorstep.

Of the three mutts Jeff was by far the most impressive. He was fit as a flea and had a rare turn of speed and he was a worthy favourite at 2–1 on. Jock, the second dog was your average mongrel, reasonably lively and at 2–1 second favourite might just shake Jeff up a bit.

The third and final entry was Dumbo, a fat friendly old thing who lolloped along at a brisk walk when he was flat out. He hadn't a snowball's chance in hell of catching Jeff? But he was everybody's favourite and by the time of the off he had been backed down from 10–1 to 9–2. In fact if there was one dog I didn't want to win it was Dumbo but I had no cause for alarm, two ton Tessie O'Shea had more chance of winning the Grand National.

The morning of the race was heralded in by the relentless tropical sun that promised to fry everyone alive by noon and everyone that wasn't on watch assembled on the beach, creating the atmosphere of a mini Epsom Downs on Derby Day. The three dog handlers took their charges a hundred yards down the beach while the spectators gathered five yards past the winning line waving bones and biscuits to encourage their fancy past the post.

The Best Laid Plans

Came the moment of truth, and I dropped my handkerchief and the handlers released the dogs with a playful slap on the rear and the punters jumped up and down and cheered like crazy, urging their fancy to supreme efforts, but the best laid plans of mice and men. . . As a race it was a non event.

As soon as he was released Jeff who loves the sea and divides his life between the beach and the cookhouse, made a beeline for the ocean and in two seconds he was revelling in it, followed immediately by Jock who was always ready for a game with Jeff. The only competitor to conform to my master plan was lovable old Dumbo, who, seeing all his friends in the distance waving hand-fuls of goodies, lolloped towards them at a steady two knots with his tongue hanging out and his tail thumping away, and a small fortune riding on his back!

The punters were ecstatic and I saw a month's pay disappear in the forty seconds it took Dumbo to flip-flop a hundred yards. They say that war produces the most unlikely heroes, but this was ridiculous.

Accra

Yet another draft appeared tantalisingly on the notice board, this time to Accra which was just a compara-tively short trip down the coast to Ghana. Paraphrasing the popular song of the moment the lads were singing, 'Would you like to go to Accra, carry bearings home in a jar?'

In all probability we'd be exchanging one hellhole for another, but we duly put in for it, working on the principle that a change was as good as a holiday. We didn't get that draft either and we were beginning to feel that we must be indispensible, but we'd put on the bottom of our application form 'Or any future draft which may occur', a comment which bought us up in front of the CO who pointed out that there were worse places than Freetown.

I was tempted to say, 'Name one!'

The Eating Contest

My next financial venture was an eating contest. There was never a shortage of food in West Africa, it was the quality that was lacking, not the quantity. Potatoes were usually rotten by the time they had reached our far-flung outpost, and any fresh vegetables were a luxury. The staple diet was soya links and red lead, which was a meatless sausage and tinned tomatoes and was a right turnoff for anyone with a sensitive palate, but was all grist that comes to the mill for starving matelots.

So when (for a small consideration) I got the canteen manager to put on one side some really edible delicacies that came via NAAFI, there was a rush to enter the contest. I finally selected four gourmets and was lucky enough to find a likely candidate from each country in the British Isles and behold we had an international contest.

Then we got around to the object of the exercise and I opened my book. The even money favourite was Butch from England. His form was there for all to see. He weighed around seventeen stone and had an appetite to match and was always going back to the galley for 'seconds'. Angus the Scot with the red beard had a reputation for putting it away and was a popular second choice at 9–4 and Taffy (no prizes for guessing his nationality was next in the betting at 4–1. The outsider at 10–1 was a beanpole of a lad from Ireland who had only been with us a month, named Carey.

They're Off!

The Ward Room contributed Lieutenant Lucan who was a particularly smooth talker to do the running commentary and we were ready to start. Well almost ready — we couldn't find the Irish champion. 'Where the hell is he?' I demanded of the assembly, and a voice from the crowd said, 'He's in the mess finishing his supper!'

I couldn't believe my ears and promptly offered him at 100–8 with no takers. Carey entered a moment later, quite unperturbed and after a brief spiel from the lieutenant, they were off.

The first round consisted of three bowls of soup with a slice of bread with each bowl, followed by a whole chicken and chips — twice! Taffy was obviously struggling by the time he had finished his second chicken and when he saw the next course of six eggs on toast arrive, he declared he was unable to go on and left the table to the accompaniment of loud boos from his backers.

The next course consisting of a whole tin of plum duff and custard saw Angus off and a red faced Butch eyed the Irish outsider suspiciously as he eagerly waded into a large tin of peaches and cream which followed it. They were nearly through a bunch of a dozen bananas when Butch clapped his hand over his mouth and rushed out of the door and to tumultous applause Lieutenant Lucan proclaimed the Irishman champion, while Carey was leaning across and taking Butch's last banana.

Plum Duff (Again)

The first prize was a small silver cup and a tin of plum duff. To the astonishment of the crowd the Irishman requested that we opened the tin as it was no good like that and helping himself to custard, he polished it off in front of his admiring fans.

How anyone could pack all that food into a frame that had a twenty-four inch waist and a chest that looked very similar will always remain a mystery, but the good news was that it was a 'Skinner' for the book and I recouped all my losses over Dumbo and quite a bit besides. I filled the table top with bottles of Black Horse and invited Benny, Bugsy and Toddy to drink up.

As a point of information no-one had told the Lieutenant that everyone there had wagered a few bob or in some cases their week's pay on the outcome of the contest and he must have been amazed how fervently they cheered their fancy and how desperate they became when he began to flag. He must have thought (not for the first time) that the ways of the lower deck are indeed strange.

The Brainstorm

Shortly after this the CO had a brainstorm. His nerves were already frayed by the antics of the terrible twins and although he had got them out of his hair, there was an unmistakable air of resentment among the rest of us. Promises had been made and had been broken, not the least of which was the fact that men who had served their allotted term of eighteen months were still here while the RAF sent their men home after nine months. Not for nothing was Sierra Leone called 'the white man's grave'. The local cemetery was filled with the victims of black water fever and malaria and while eighteen months in the Ward Room occasionally entertaining the white nurses from the hospital and eating reasonable food with the mess silver in civilized surroundings was probably a piece of cake, eighteen months on the lower deck living like a coolie was not too much fun, and morale was pretty low.

The CO's solution to the problem was to aggravate it even further. He decided in his wisdom that we needed more discipline and the whole ship was to become 'shipshape and Bristol fashion' and to achieve this all men who came off the middle watch would parade for one hour's drill at noon the following day complete with full tropical uniform boots and all and carrying a rifle!

We were dumbfounded. He was getting pretty good results when we were on watch and none of us had ever had a complete day off since we'd been there and now this.

'Go Slow'

We held unofficial talks in the huts and decided that although we wouldn't mess up the watchkeeping, for that would endanger the lives of our men at sea, everything else would be a campaign of 'go slow' and dumb insolence. I figured that a week of that would drive them up the wall.

We had acquired a goat that had become the ship's mascot (I think the old man had seen a film of one of the guards regiments and thought it would be a status symbol) and the CO would parade it whenever he had the slightest opportunity such as Trafalgar Day or in his case when Mafeking was relieved I shouldn't wonder. Anyway, someone who shall be nameless (and it wasn't yours truly) clipped the beard off the mascot and hung it over the entrance to the camp with the message 'Abandon hope all ye that enter here!' which considering we were staggering about with rifles in the noonday sun, having been up half the night, just about summed up our situation.

Mutiny

That message coupled with our little campaign — which was already driving the officers and the Chief up the wall — was the last straw. The CO called the entire ship's company together other than the watch keepers and read us the riot act — literally.

He fixed his beady eye on me and said we were

perilously close to mutiny and read out the penalties of same, not the least of which was being shot. I switched my gaze to the Chief and found his eyes boring in on me as well. At last the CO cooled down and said in a stern voice, 'Do you understand all I've said?'

I knew he expected some response from us and I guessed the Chief had probably suggested to him that I was most likely one of the ringleaders so firmly believing that attack is the best form of defense I took my courage in both hands and stoo up. 'I am sure I speak for all of us here when I say we have no intention of mutiny, sir, but if you want to maintain an efficient ship we can't possibly carry on drilling in the heat of the day when we should be resting. The men will be breaking down, sir'.

Captain Bligh

I think by now he had begun to realise the same thing, that he would be short of watchkeepers if he didn't change tack, so he gazed on us much as Captain Bligh must have gazed on the crew of the Bounty just before they changed places and said in a low threatening voice, 'Very well, I think you have learned your lesson and I am prepared to be magnaminous and return to normal routine, but if there are any more breaches of discipline, I will have the culprits up on a court martial'. He turned to Stevenson, 'Carry on, Chief' and strode from the room.

Back in the hut we were jubilant, we had no doubt who had won and back in the Ward Room was a very relieved skipper who had averted a major blot on his copybook by the skin of his teeth. It's always rather difficult to get promoted once you've had your ship's company mutiny on you.

to and then that angel of mercy th[...]
whistle. It was the only sporting [...]
taken part in that I was pleased to [...]
first round!

The Filibuster

With the return to normal routin[...]
tween us and the management i[...]
and we were soon back to a rea[...]
ence, or more precisely makin[...]
posting.

One evening we were having [...]
sion in the canteen, the centre pi[...]
being the measurements of a cert[...]
all known back in the halcyon d[...]
as the debate reached a crescen[...]
the figures of 42 and 44 were b[...]
although the same age as ours[...]
elder statesman, called us all t[...]
chair' he shouted above the h[...]
restored some kind of order.

'You can't all speak at once[...]
seems to me that Dave (yours tr[...]
most to say, and I suggest we let [...]
systems, then we can all join in'.[...]

The lads quickly worked out a [...]
fairly straightforward. They sat [...]
a bottle of Black Horse at our el[...]
had to talk continuously for on[...]
ping, when we would be allowe[...]
as much beer as we could and th[...]
beer was free to the winner bu[...]
own. I readily agreed as it seem[...]
and Fred was just as keen.

We went over to hut two with a couple of bottles of beer to offer to Ferby. Why Ferby? Well, he was seen the night before standing by the goat with a pair of scissors in his hand.

The Swimming Gala

Our skipper was not usually motivated to do anything that didn't produce bigger and better bearings on U-boats but obviously someone had suggested that something should be done to show that all had been forgiven and the following Saturday they organised an impromptu swimming gala (if that's not a contradiction of terms) at the cove by the cape, which was ideal because it contained three fathoms of reasonably safe, clear water.

Swimming is not my long suit, in fact I swim better under water than on top of it — I don't swallow so much — but I loved high diving and springboards. Not that I had elegance and poise, I just found it exhilarating flying through the air, and so I managed a third place in the high diving by sheer enthusiasm.

The swimming events had me thrashing about with the also rans, even Gus finished in front of me which was the ultimate embarrassment, but eventually they held an event in which I really fancied my chances — the greasy pole!

It didn't have quite the status of the two hundred yards crawl, but it could wipe out the memories of my ignominious failures in the swimming events. The first couple of rounds were no problem but I met Benny in the semi-final and we had a rare tussle before he eventually over-reached himself and skidded off the pole into the sea.

The Sledgehammer

On paper the final looked lik
nent was well over six feet t
and a half stone, but he drev
end of the pole which was sl
cially with his weight and o
much more stable in such a s

That was the credit side, or
his pillow like a sledgeham
punishment before I manage
blockbusters and as he follov
round the side of the head an

David had beaten Goliath

Water Polo

The final event of the day wa
and I stupidly allowed myse
goalkeeper on account of t
involved. No swimming? I g
and once their forwards atta
me. A fierce throw sent the
and I parried it and then pou
away. As I seized it their stri
giant I'd just beaten on the
stretched out a huge paw a
water. I came up still clutch
came down on my head on
This time I got the messag
surfaced coughing and splut
back of the net and my tor
gratulations of his teammate

This procedure was repe
sions, plus two more goals th

To the producer of 'Just a Minute' the radio show that was a hit long after the war, I would say, 'there's nothing new under the sun'.

The contest started in a fairly civilized manner, we both babbled about everything from boobs to bibles and ten minutes later we were still going strong, aided and abetted by the Black Horse. Fred was proving a tough nut to crack and after twenty minutes when I was expounding on the beauty and reliability of the 69 trolleybus that plied for trade down Tottenham High Street and Fred was burbling on about that exotic dish the Lancashire hotpot, that he began to falter. There is only so much you can say about a Lancashire hotpot and he was running out of ideas and he was half cut.

Worried Sponsors

'Tell us what's wrong with the navy' came a suggestion from the crowd and I seized on it and was away on my favourite hobby horse. Five minutes later Fred was done with and slumped exhausted in his chair while they fished the price of seven bottles of Black Horse from his pocket.

Meanwhile I had the bit between my teeth and was expounding on my policy for a perfect navy. The drunker I became the more I talked ... and talked ... and talked and the sponsors were becoming increasing uneasy about the mess bill.

An hour later and I was still drinking and babbling and in desperation they tied me to a chair and dumped me outside, clutching a new bottle of Black Horse, but a curious crowd gathered around me in the moonlight and I barely paused.

They looked at Toddy who had unleashed this torrent

We went over to hut two with a couple of bottles of beer to offer to Ferby. Why Ferby? Well, he was seen the night before standing by the goat with a pair of scissors in his hand.

The Swimming Gala

Our skipper was not usually motivated to do anything that didn't produce bigger and better bearings on U-boats but obviously someone had suggested that something should be done to show that all had been forgiven and the following Saturday they organised an impromptu swimming gala (if that's not a contradiction of terms) at the cove by the cape, which was ideal because it contained three fathoms of reasonably safe, clear water.

Swimming is not my long suit, in fact I swim better under water than on top of it — I don't swallow so much — but I loved high diving and springboards. Not that I had elegance and poise, I just found it exhilarating flying through the air, and so I managed a third place in the high diving by sheer enthusiasm.

The swimming events had me thrashing about with the also rans, even Gus finished in front of me which was the ultimate embarrassment, but eventually they held an event in which I really fancied my chances — the greasy pole!

It didn't have quite the status of the two hundred yards crawl, but it could wipe out the memories of my ignominious failures in the swimming events. The first couple of rounds were no problem but I met Benny in the semi-final and we had a rare tussle before he eventually over-reached himself and skidded off the pole into the sea.

The Sledgehammer

On paper the final looked like a 'no contest'. My oppo-
nent was well over six feet tall and weighed fourteen
and a half stone, but he drew the outside berth on the
end of the pole which was slightly more springy, especially with his weight and of course a smaller chap is
much more stable in such a situation than a large one.

That was the credit side, on the debit side he wielded
his pillow like a sledgehammer and I took some rare
punishment before I managed to duck under one of his
blockbusters and as he followed through I caught him
round the side of the head and he toppled over and out.

David had beaten Goliath again!

Water Polo

The final event of the day was a water polo tournament
and I stupidly allowed myself to be talked into playing
goalkeeper on account of there being no swimming
involved. No swimming? I got tired just treading water
and once their forwards attacked I wondered what hit
me. A fierce throw sent the ball hurtling towards me
and I parried it and then pounced on the ball as it spun
away. As I seized it their striker (who I realised was the
giant I'd just beaten on the greasy pole — who else?)
stretched out a huge paw and pushed me under the
water. I came up still clutching the ball and the paw
came down on my head once again and held it there.
This time I got the message and let go the ball and
surfaced coughing and spluttering to see the ball in the
back of the net and my tormentor receiving the congratulations of his teammates.

This procedure was repeated on three more occasions, plus two more goals that I never even got a hand

of words on the unsuspecting world and asked if he'd got any more bright ideas. 'Why not take him over to the War Room', he suggested, 'I'm sure they'd like to know where Winston went wrong'.

I was duly carted over to the Holy of Holies, still ranting on and still swigging my source of inspiration, the Black Horse. Toddy respectfully knocked on the door and Lucan came out to see what all the commotion was about.

'It's Windsor, sir', said Toddy, 'we can't stop him talking.'

Lucan grinned and said, 'Two of you bring him in and we'll have a look'. I was dumped still tied to my chair in front of a curious semi-circle of officers and without pausing continued my soliloquy on my policy for the perfect navy, although with hindsight there may have been some flaws in the theory. Not every admiral should necessarily be born in the East End of London, for example.

They listened enthralled (or something like that) for some twenty minutes or so until the novelty wore off and as I showed no signs of slackening, and my bottle was nearly empty, Lucan stood up and with a wry smile said, 'All right, Todd, get rid of him'.

'But how do we shut him up, sir?' asked Toddy.

'You take him over to the ablutions, sit him under a shower and turn it on', said the lieutenant. 'If that doesn't shut him up, nothing will'.

I was duly carried over to the heads and the prescribed remedy was carried out forthwith and was an instant success. No filibuster could cope with such adverse conditions and my policy collapsed and so did I.

They carted me back to the hut, untied me and stripped off my sodden clothes, gave me a brisk rub down, pushed me under my mosquito net and draped a blanket over me and I fell straight into a drunken slumber.

As Toddy said the next day, 'All I did was call the meeting to order. . .'

Our Soccer Team

Although we were only a small unit compared to the main Army, Navy and Air Force barracks (Kissi could muster 2,000 men) we had an extraordinary percentage of good footballers amongst us, and could give anyone in Sierra Leone a run for their money. There was a very old, bald-headed chap named Little (who was actually 34) who had apparently been on the books of Bolton Wanderers before he had a better offer from HM's Government, and our skipper Scattergood (Scatters for short) was reputed to have Notts Forest chasing him, but they'd have to wait until Hitler stopped chasing him first.

Benny, Bugsie and myself were all of a reasonable amateur club standard, my claim to fame was that after the war I signed on for Enfield Town who in 1947 were one of the leading lights in the Athenium League. To be truthful I played for the stiffs (the reserves) and the first team man I was trying to replace was playing for England and was light years ahead of me, so my first team appearances were limited to the end of the season when, because the team were doing well, they became so involved that they couldn't cope with all their fixtures and they used us in all the minor cup fixtures until it got to the quarter or semi-finals when they turned out the big guns.

Still it was nice to pull on a first team shirt on those rare occasions and to the small boys who didn't know any different, I was a bit of a hero. I was always the great pretender. At the end of the season a pal of mine in the reserves said he had been offered a few bob to play in the Edmonton Sunday Premier League by a team who shall be nameless as it was strictly illegal, and was I interested? I was and it was adios to Enfield Town.

But all this is a far cry from the sun-baked pitches of Africa where the lads of Aberdeen were making ripples on the Sierra Leone football circles as we finished runners-up to Kissi in the navy league, only one point behind and then following a good run in the Inter-Services Cup, we were due to meet our old adversary the main naval barracks in the semi-final.

The Yellow Brick Wall

Came the big day and with a lorry load of special operators in support we launched ourselves at the opposition and from my totally unbiased viewpoint, we rang rings round them — until we reached the penalty area when we came up against their secret weapon in the shape of a huge goalie named Brown. Rumour had it he played for Scotland and I could well believe it. He wore a yellow jersey and it was like kicking against a yellow brick wall.

Everything in that area was His with a capital 'H' and, of course, the inevitable happened, they broke away and scored the only goal of the match. I can still see my chance to have been the hero of the day when, with twenty minutes to go I broke free of their defense and let fly from ten yards out. It was going for the top left hand corner and looked good, but a huge paw stretched out for the umpteenth time and pushed it round the post. Two minutes later they went ahead.

'Snowball'

It was the end of a dream, for our team broke up the following season for various reasons and we were a shadow of our former selves, but at least it gave us another purpose in life other than watchkeeping and helped the weeks to fly by during the season.

I can't mention football without including the native Sierra Leone team and in particular a character called 'Snowball'. Anyone who watched them play during the war will know immediately to whom I am referring. He had a shock of white hair, played in bare feet (as did most of the team) and was tricky as a wagon load of monkeys. He would have filled many a stadium at home but of course he never got the chance and we'll never know how good he was. I would think he'd reached his peak when I saw him as he was at least thirty and from then on it was all down hill, but he was certainly a big fish in a small pool and the West Africans worshipped him. Are you still out there, Snowball, or have you melted away?

Gabby

We had served about a year of our time when Owen arrived. He said he was a schoolteacher from Cardiff but he had 'bent' written all over him and I would have had severe reservations about leaving any kids of mine in his loving care.

He soon struck up a relationship with 'Gabby', a civilian lorry driver of about my own age who lived in a village some five miles away. Most of the natives had a quiet dignity which could sometimes embarrass you when you saw our lads on a run ashore behaving like animals.

Gabby had no such pretensions. He was cocky, arrogant and a con man to boot and just the sight of him was enough to wind me up. Owen was soon captivated by this witty (Gabby was never lost for words) and what seemed to him, physically attractive driver. He showered upon him gifts of rings, watches and baubles of all kinds which Gabby always delighted in displaying to our little gang knowing full well the effect it would have on us. A red flag to a bull would have seemed pale pink compared to Benny's reactions.

Adoption

The last straw came when Gabby announced that Owen was taking him back to Wales when the war was over and would adopt him. At first we were speechless and then we rushed off to find Owen to confirm or deny this outrageous boast of Gabby's. Our worst fears were immediately confirmed and we tried our damndest to talk him out of it from common sense (which as Owen proved is not so common) to the hard facts of life mentioning such details as Gabby was a money-grabbing, untrustworthy son of a bitch, but it was all to no avail.

'Do-gooders' were unheard of in those days and Owen was about twenty years ahead of his time. The race relations board was not even a sick joke during the war years and it was perfectly possible to say unkind things about coloured people without ending up in court. All of which meant that Gabby and Owen were in for a hard time when they arrived in the U.K. There was no question of 'keeping a welcome in the hillside', but the Welshman was adamant — Gabby deserved a chance to develop his talents.

Lovelorn

They almost deserved each other, Owen with his lecherous intentions and Gabby with his eye on the main chance to get a British passport, take Owen for every penny he possessed and then scarper. All this we pointed out to the lovelorn schoolteacher, but he would have none of it. Love is indeed blind.

The next day we had a soccer match against an army team and Gabby was detailed to drive us there. We sat in the back of his open lorry and a Sublieutenant Morrow who had only been out in Sierra Leone some three weeks, sat beside the driver. We had a great game, beating them 3–2 with 'old man' Little scoring the winner three minutes from time, and we were in great spirits as we piled back into the lorry.

High as a Kite

Gabby was waiting in the driver's seat and at the word of command roared up the road at about eighty m.p.h., which for a clapped out navy truck is a rare old speed. What we didn't know was that during the two hours he had been waiting for us, he had pawned his 'adoption present' over the bar in the village and drunk the proceeds. Consequently, he was high as a kite. After nearly leaving the road on a couple of bends the lads in the front began to bang on the roof of the cab and even the officer began to realise that all was not well.

He sharply ordered Gabby to stop the lorry, which he reluctantly did and then he ordered the driver out of the cab, at which point Owen's pet dug his heels in, shouting 'This is Gabby's lorry! Gabby's lorry!'

The sub then called for two men to shift the driver and gave him a helpful push. The effect on Gabby was electric, he jumped out of the cab before the volunteers could get down and had reached the officer just as he dismounted from the other side. He whipped out a twelve inch knife and pinning the sub against the cab, brandished it in his face.

Providence Smiles

Fred, who was the first to arrive, grabbed his wrist, but Gabby had gone berserk, the adrenalin was flowing and he was proving a rare handful. By this time the lorry was half empty and providence smiled on me. There lying behind the cab was the starting handle. With great presence of mind and without an evil thought in my head, I picked it up and leaned over the officer and gave Gabby a sharp tap on the head — purely in the course of duty you understand.

He collapsed in a heap on the road and Sublieutenant Morrow's expression changed from one of gratitude to apprehension. The last thing he needed was a dead driver.

The Good News

He need not have worried. We tossed Gabby in the back of the lorry and one of the lads took over the wheel and after ten minutes, assisted by a filthy bucket of water from a ditch, Gabby moaned and opened his eyes. I showed him the starting handle as a reminder, but all the fight had gone out of him and he lay on the floor for the rest of the journey back to camp, groaning and dabbing his head.

The good news was that Gabby lost his job and was forbidden to come back to the camp ever again, while the Chief who knew what the score was, had a word with Owen and said he would prefer charges if he ever went looking for his lost love.

Owen was crestfallen but he got the message and that was the end of a beautiful friendship.

The Mile

Noel Coward had a point about 'mad dogs and English-men' for in spite of the intense heat we never missed an opportunity to take up every available sporting chal-lenge. The naval sports meeting was held in 1944 as a sure sign that the pressure from the Germans was less-ening in West Africa. Egged on my my so-called mates, I entered the mile event which used to be my forte and promptly regretted it. Instead of pounding in my bunk, our killick 'hard hearted Mac' would have me pound-ing up and down Lumley beach every day until I was fit to drop.

As Bugsie remarked when Mac hung his blanket out to air, 'You can see what he does for exercise'. We counted twenty-eight separate stains on it which Mac claimed were 'wet dreams' and while a few of them may well have been, we reckoned that three quarters of them were self induced. All of which meant that Mac was in no fit state to accompany me on my training runs, but he would sit on the beach with a bottle of Black Horse while I ran till I was a speck in the distance, then he would raise his arm and I would sprint back as fast as I could, which earned me a swig out of the bottle. It was pretty unorthodox but nevertheless, when the great day came I was in pretty good shape. The race went pretty well according to my plan as I dropped in behind the pacemaker and after three laps I was feeling pretty comfortable. With fifty yards to go I sprinted past him and made for home and the winner's rostrum where all the best heroes pose. With less than twenty yards to go, there was a noise like an express train and a huge body thundered past to beat me by three yards!

The Sacrifice

I can't remember his name, but I do remember he was pretty useful and when the following month the inter-services sports were held we were both selected to represent the navy. Ten minutes before the race he took me on one side and said, 'I don't like to ask you this but I know if someone sets a good pace I can win this — would you mind?'

What could I say? 'That my mates had turned up to watch me, not him', but put like that it made sense. I knew I had no chance of beating him, and I was there to run for the 'Andrew' not for me, so rather sadly I agreed to become his human sacrifice.

As good as my word I sprinted off from the very word 'go' and was soon joined by an RAF corporal for which I was truly thankful (he'd probably been given similar instructions from his sergeant) and for three and a half laps we were locked in battle, towing the rest of the field behind us.

Eventually the expected RAF man and a squaddie edged past us and with thirty yards to go I was anxiously looking for my man. I needn't have worried, he was an expert and with his usual devastating finish, he swept by them as though they weren't there. I staggered in, in fourth place just two yards behind the RAF and the Army champs with a sneaking suspicion that I could have been a lot closer if I'd run my own race, but he was waiting for me as I passed the tape and grabbed me in a bear hug and swept me off my feet. 'We've done it', he roared. 'Well run, me old mate' and never a one to spurn reflected glory, I let him raise my arm with his and we jogged over to the navy supporters.

Once in a Lifetime

To me the highlight of the afternoon was the performance of a member of the West African Frontier Force. The natives had their own sports meeting alternating with our events (who said Apartheid?) and I watched disinterestedly as this unimpressive looking character won the 100 yards sprint. He also won the 100 yards hurdles and I still wasn't taking much notice when he won the 220 yards.

When he took the 440 there was a mild buzz among the spectators and when he lined up for the 880 all eyes were upon him. Naturally he won and fifteen minutes later he's there in the line up for the mile, which not surprisingly he won also.

There was only one track event left, the five miles. Surely he won't? But he did and came home alone waving his arms in the air to his mates. It was a performance the like of which you'll see only once in a lifetime, and completely unforgettable. His name? I haven't a clue except it was quite unpronounceable, but I'll wager his grandfather used to carry messages for hundreds of miles in a cleft stick.

Cockles' Letter

One day a letter that was definitely different arrived for me. It was postmarked South Africa and the sender was none other than my bosom pal of yesteryear 'Cockles'. Apparently he was completing his training as a pilot and even more apparently he was having the time of his life. 'But hold on a minute', I thought, 'this is 1944 and he's still training. What happened to 1942 and 1943?'

As if in answer to my silent query the letter went on, 'As you know, I'm a bit younger than you (six months) and by the time I was on the volunteer reserve they were innundated with potential air crew and when I finally got in they had more than they knew what to do with — or shall I say more than they could cope with because of a shortage of trainer planes.

'Eventually they sent me to Canada and now I'm in Jo'berg and if all goes well I'll have my wings in a couple of months, which brings me to the point of this letter. When this course ends, I've got some leave due and you've been out in that dump so long you surely must have some to come as well, so seeing as we are both in Africa why don't we meet up? I've had a look at the map and I thought Victoria Falls was about half way, so what do y'think?'

Oh, Cockles! While Victoria Falls may seem just up the road to the RAF, it's about two months' sailing from Freetown, even if I could get the leave, which was out of the question (not to mention the boat) but it's the thought that counts and I was certainly pleased to hear from him and we agreed to postpone our rendezvous until after the war, or at any rate until there wasn't three thousand miles between us.

It occurred to me that if Cockles was going to become a hero, he was cutting it a bit fine.

The Epidemic

The mosquitos which were always with us were particularly active of late and woe betide the matelot who found one inside his mosquito net when he awoke. First you said a prayer that it was a male for only the female can give you malaria (I will refrain from making comparisons with the females of other species) and simply say that the next move was to swat the little blighter and if blood came out of it, you went straight down to the sick bay for an extra dose of quinine.

This was later changed to mephachrin tablets which although easier to distribute to the troops had the unfortunate side effect of turning your skin yellow. If we'd been fighting the Japs they'd have been right confused. Soon two or three of the lads went down with Malaria and then for good measure the camp was struck by an epidemic of dysentry. It was chaotic, the heads were full and the men were dashing into the bush in all directions. Watchkeeping became a nightmare and on the second night half of us were bundled into lorries and sent off to Freetown General Hospital, including yours truly who had managed to get both malaria and dysentry at the same time.

If ever you're not sure whether you want to die or not, I recommend this little double dose. The end of the world would be a blessed release from that lot.

On the Mend

For over a week I sweated pints with a temperature that I'd only produced before when watching Bridget Bardot. In between I crawled to the loos which were always overcrowded and prayed for oblivion.

Eventually I came round and began to feel more like my old self and once I began to mend I realised that this was about the closest I had been to paradise for a very long time. The food was a thousand per cent better than anything at the camp, we had clean sheets and were tended by white nurses and I realised that I hadn't spoken to a white girl for over a year — and there was no watchkeeping!

I'd just had my first time off in yonks and I'd missed it!

It was then that I realised the occupants at the other end of the ward were different from us and on a closer inspection they turned out to be Italian POWs. Dysentry doesn't discriminate.

The Challenge

We were lying on our beds that night feeling shattered but happy when there was a thunder of flatulation from the Wops' end of the ward. The echo had barely died away when the challenge was taken up by a matelot in a bed across the way. An even louder clap came from the Italian end followed again by retaliation from the bed opposite. The Italian started on his third run with great gusto but it finished in a horrible gurgle as the inevitable happened and he dashed from the ward. The moral being, 'You can't take liberties with dysentry'.

There is a serpent in every paradise and mine was down the other end of the ward, as I contemplated the irony of the fact that the only enemy I'd ever seen at close quarters were already prisoners.

The hospital had obviously been told that we were needed back urgently, as indeed we were for it must have been chaotic back at Aberdeen with only half the ship's company to cover the entire North and South Atlantic. They worked extra watches and abandoned some of the more northern frequencies, but obviously they couldn't keep that up indefinitely and inevitably within two days of coming round I was on the lorry back to camp with half a dozen others and most of the lads were back within two or three days of that. At the end of the week we all did a couple of extra watches to give the lads who had held the fort a break — they needed it!

The Bank Manager

At the far end of our hut the bunk opposite Mac was occupied by Anthony (not 'Tony' old boy, if you don't mind). He came from a middle-class background and in civvy street he had been a remarkably young bank manager at the age of thirty-four. What he was doing as an ordinary member of the lower deck was a complete mystery to us and Anthony was anything but forthcoming on the subject. We speculated that he'd blotted his copy book in a big way at home and joined up in a hurry — something like joining the foreign legion, only he was lucky there was a war on and he could be amongst Brits.

He didn't mix too well with the rest of us, which was hardly surprising as he spoke with a plum in his mouth and couldn't really relate to our life-style at home any more than we could relate to his.

He'd already served his eighteen months out here but showed no inclination to push for a chittie back to Merry England. In fact, the reverse was true, he was prepared to sit out the entire war on the edge of a mangove swamp.

The Alarm Clock

We first noticed that there was something radically wrong with Anthony when he smuggled in a small alarm clock which he always set for three a.m. or five thirty if he was on the middle watch.

Fortunately, he was at the other end of the hut to Benny and the muffled sound rarely disturbed us — it was just enough to wake the owner. But why, you are asking would anyone want to wake up in the middle of a perfectly good night's sleep?

A good question, and the answer came in the form of a bottle chinking on a glass immediately after the alarm went off. We all knew Anthony had a drink problem, but this was ridiculous — he couldn't bear to sleep the whole night through without a drink.

Like most alcoholics he managed to get through his job without it being too obvious, but I often wondered how many U-boats got away because of Anthony. He was never short of funds because Daddy used to send him a monthly allowance, which had he realised the life style he was helping his son to maintain, he would have been horrified, for not only was Anthony a drunk but for good measure he had 'gone native'.

Sex and Booze

He had found himself a buxom young mistress in the village and half of his allowance was spent on Western style clothes for the lady and the rest on booze. Not surprisingly he spent nearly all his spare time in a mud hut with a corrugated iron roof, which was a far cry from his home in the stockbroker belt south of London.

The relationship had been going on for over a year and presumably had been set up when Anthony had 'all his marbles' for they had a complete understanding. He gave her a lifestyle that was way above that of anyone else in the village and she knew which side her bread was buttered and was completely faithful to him, which was just as well for Anthony could ill afford a dose of the clap to add to his other problems.

I think someone tipped the CPO off about the wealthiest member of the lower deck, for three weeks later a reluctant Anthony was shipped off to the UK leaving behind the love of his life (well, second love of his life actually) — he was still clutching a bottle as the lorry swept out of the gate.

What his unsuspecting parents would make of him when he arrived home I dread to think — or perhaps the police picked him up first.

Dogged

By now Stevenson the Chief had begun to believe he was the skipper and threw his weight around at the slightest provocation — or even without provocation. One particularly nasty incident personified the man and gave him my vote as 'Bastard of the Year'.

Two of the dogs in my ill-fated race had disappeared and only 'Dumbo' remained on the camp. They had probably gone off on safari and Dumbo knowing his limitations and not being at all dumb, stayed put. About this time another mongrel turned up, he was a friendly, lively little thing and he won the heart of Mick in hut three.

Mick was a loner who was the biggest nonentity I ever knew and I could imagine his horror when he got his calling up papers, to be thrust into a cauldron of life when all he wanted was his clerk's job in a tiny office and his radio in the evenings. He had no real friends and was the butt of any bully wherever he went, but we used to keep an eye on him so that life was reasonably tolerable for him at Aberdeen.

The Chief got wind of the fact that Mick had acquired another dog and being a natural bully, it was with considerable relish that he called him in to his office.

'I hear you've got a dog', he said in a soft, yet menacing voice.

'Yes, Chief', came the answer. 'Well, we've just got rid of two and we've got quite enough with bloody Dumbo — and the sooner he goes the better — so get rid of it, OK?'

'But, Chief', Mick began. 'No buts, I'm ordering you to get rid of it. Dismiss!'

Mick was shattered. He sat on the steps of his hut cuddling 'Pickin' his new (and only) friend with tears in his eyes. He just couldn't bring himself to part with him and that night made him a bed as usual behind the hut.

Pistol-Packer

For two days he kept Pickin out of Sevenson's sight but on the third day the Chief was making an unexpected detour to the 'Kroo' quarters when he stumbled upon the pair of them together at the back of the hut.

'Fetch that mutt round to my office', he barked and was waiting outside when Mick and his best friend arrived, followed by some half a dozen curious sightseers. To Mick's horror the Chief was holding a pistol for obvious reasons.

'I told you three days ago that you'd got to get rid of that dog', he roared. 'That was an order and you saw fit to disobey it, so now you must take the consequences!'

'Don't shoot him, Chief,' begged Mick.

"I wouldn't dream of it', came the reply. 'I'm not going to shoot him, you are!' and he thrust the gun into Mick's hands and the lad burst into tears.

'I can't', he sobbed. 'Then let me help you', said the Chief and he closed his hand round Mick's, took aim and squeezed the trigger. Fortunately it was all over in an instant and Pickin was no more.

Someone at the back of the crowd called out, 'You filthy bastard', and the Chief knowing he would never find out who it was gave a steely smile and said to Mick who was now on his knees by the corpse, crying bitterly, 'Now bury it!'

If there was any doubt in our minds who was the most hated man in the entire ship's company, that settled it. He took over from Al Capone as our contemporary 'Public enemy number one'.

E.S.P.

Some things you can't explain and I've never really believed in mediums, extra sensory perception and the like, but I had to admit to a severe dose of something of that ilk when I stood on parade one Sunday morning prior to a church service to be conducted by the visiting padre from the main barracks.

It happened once a month and if he thought he was doing us a favour, then I've got news for him. When you've been up half the night you need a parade and a church service like a hole in the head, but if the powers that be decided my soul needed saving, then who is this miserable sinner to defy the almighty, especially when he's dressed in his best Chief's uniform.

It was indeed a far cry from the days when I would voluntarily run to the Boys' Brigade Bible Class to soak up every word and sing with gusto and really believe. The navy was turning me into a cynic.

Behind us as we stood on parade some workmen were erecting a new monument to our skipper in the form of a 100 foot tower which would greatly improve our reception — and being Sunday you can bet they were on time and a half. Mac our killick had got us nicely lined up and was giving us the once over before the chief arrived when I felt an overwhelming desire to break ranks.

It was crazy but in that split second a tremendous tug of war took place in my mind. What for? Why? Tell 'em you're sick! and before I knew it I had taken a smart step forward. Even as I stood there and before I had time to feel the complete idiot that I should have, a bolt that had slipped from the workman's hands some 80 feet above crashed down onto the very spot where I had been standing.

Mac always the master of understatement, nonchalently picked it up and said casually, 'Close, wasn't it?'

No action was taken against the workman, and I wouldn't have wished it. He was profuse with his apologies and it was in no way deliberate and apart from his foreman bending his ear, the matter was closed on the spot without an enquiry.

Back in the hut I was trying to convince them that I had special powers but Benny came up with a more practical theory. 'You probably heard the bolt whizzing down and even though you don't know where it's going to land, your instinct makes you move somewhere — anywhere, you just cannot stand still and wait and see what happens'. Well, maybe I did at that!

Monkey Business

The tower was duly completed and stood there not surprisingly towering over our camp. It had been there only two weeks when out of the bush appeared a troop of monkeys who were obviously attracted by our super of monkeys who were obviously attracted by our super tree.

Quickly the leader jumped onto the lower bars and with a dozen or so following behind, he began scaling the tower intent on reaching the aerial. The duty officer appeared among the onlookers and called for a volunteer to shift them. He need not have bothered for the words were barely out of his mouth before 'Nobby' Clark, the only seaman in the ship's company, was on the bottom rung and began climbing steadily.

The monkeys would not come down and the higher Nobby climbed the higher they went until they were all clustered round the top. This was a particularly nasty moment for no-one knew what their reaction would be once they were cornered and I wouldn't fancy Nobby's chances playing away from home against that little lot.

They turned and chattered and screamed at him and then at the crucial moment the leader leapt from the top with arms and legs whirling like a windmill. He seemed to be in the air for ages and it appeared impossible that he could survive a jump from that height, but to our amazement he barely paused on landing and scampered off into the bush.

The entire troop followed him without a single casualty I'm happy to say, and it certainly gave a new dimension to monkeys as far as I was concerned. Flying monkeys! Wow!

We gathered at the foot of the tower to congratulate Nobby on a sterling performance and Toddy summed it up when he observed that it took a lot of bottle to climb up there. Nobby just grinned and said, 'If you've ever been a boy sailor climbing up the mast at the Gangees with a matelot wielding a knotted rope hitting you up the arse if you faltered, anything else is a piece of cake'.

The E.C.

As I have previously mentioned, Freetown Harbour was immense. In fact it is the second largest after Rio de Janiero and at the height of the war two hundred and fifty ships, including the Queen Elizabeth and the Queen Mary were anchored at the same time. The pressure had eased off slightly but the harbour still accommodated three old hulks that had seen better days and were used as depot and supply ships. They at least were guaranteed to still be afloat at the end of the war for they never moved. The names of these three old ladies were 'The City of Tokyo', the 'Philoctetes' and last but by no means least, the notorious 'Edinburgh Castle'.

Toddy wanted a new 'tiddly suit' (which is your special outfit for going ashore and usually accompanied by gold badges as opposed to the red badges on your number threes, which is your working suit) because we were getting near the end of our allotted span of eighteen months in Sierra Leone and if promises meant anything, we would soon be on our way home. Me, I preferred to keep my cash until I was back in Chatham and in any case your clothes soon went mouldy out here.

So here we were boarding the 'Philoctetes' in search of the ship's tailor who was reputedly 'the best'. It was quite a journey from Aberdeen but it made a nice break to see how the other half of the world lived — and believe me it was another world down there.

The shanty town down by the waterside was one of the worst slums you could ever see and the three ships made an appropriate background to it. We soon found the tailor, a very efficient gent who gave the impression he had connections in Savile Row and indeed he may have been just that, for he took Toddy's measurements, said the suit would be ready next week and when the lad went back for it (I couldn't accompany him as I had to stand in on Fred's watch) it fitted like a glove without the slightest alteration — Montague Burton, eat your heart out!

Leaving the 'Philoctetes' after Toddy's measurements, we boarded the notorious 'Edinburgh Castle' and we were halfway round our tour of inspection when a suspicious Chief asked us what we were doing aboard. He didn't swallow my spontaneous fib that we were looking for the ship's tailor and sent us packing with a flea in our ear, but we'd seen enough to know that life on the E.C. was pretty grim, though fortunately most of the inmates were only there for a week or so at a time until their next ship comes along.

At the end of the war they towed her out into the South Atlantic and scuttled her and thousands of matelots lined the banks to cheer her on her way to the cries of 'Bloody good riddance!'

Leicester Peak

Our eighteen months duly came and went and it was clear that Toddy had been a trifle premature in ordering his tiddly suit, but we did get a week excused duty which was better than nothing. Of course, there was nowhere to go except Freetown, but Bugsie had a preference for the wide open spaces and suggested I accompanied him on a trip to the hills.

There were two impressive eminences dominating the skyline around Freetown, one was the Sugar Loaf Mountain and the second was Leicester Peak. Bugsie chose the latter as there was an army camp at the foot of it and we had a pretty good chance of hitching a lift there.

I should have known better than to venture into the

wilds with Bugsie, for you don't get christened with a name like that, you have to earn it and he had done just that within a month of arriving in Africa. He was absolutely captivated by the variety of creepy crawlies that were everywhere in abundance and all totally new to us. They soon became his hobby and his collection of butterflies was probably the finest in West Africa.

He never went anywhere without his hyperdermic syringe and his specimens were injected on the spot and taken lovingly back to be pinned on a huge board. I once witnessed a dour struggle between him and a scorpion that Bugsie had managed to get into an empty baked bean can. The problem was that every time Bugsie got his needle into position the scorpion lashed out with his tail at Bugsie's finger. Eventually Bugsie got the winning shot, but it was a photo finish.

So here we were at the foot of Leicester Peak after successfully catching a lorry. It is fairly easy for servicemen to be picked up by service lorries of whatever denomination when you are in a military zone, and with a grateful wave to the driver we started up a steep path that led to the top of the peak with Bugsie in the vanguard.

Black Mamba

We spent a pleasant hour or so chasing butterflies and bugs, not that I had the slightest intention of picking any of them up. Bullets I felt I could cope with, bugs are something else. We were three quarters of the way to the top when Bugsie stopped, I looked over his shoulder and I stopped too, for I didn't like that I saw one little bit. There right in the middle of the path was a black mamba, probably the most deadly snake in the world, well certainly in the Premier Division.

Its head was slightly raised but it hadn't yet been roused to fighting pitch. Perhaps it had just woken up, for they are reputed to be among the fastest of snakes on top of their other assets. It never had a chance to show its prowess for in a split second Bugsie had leaped forward, struck it round the side of its head and trapped its neck with a Y-shaped stick he always carried for just such an occasion. Gently but firmly he pressed until all the life had been squeezed out of the mamba — 'I don't want to damage the skin', he explained.

Me, I rolled my eyes in disbelief, by all the laws of nature and all the manuals I had read, it should be Bugsie lying there dead, not the snake. 'You crazy basket', I breathed slapping him on the back with relief.

Bugsie was drooling. 'What a piece of luck', he purred. 'Luck' was hardly the word for it! He stuffed the snake inside his shirt 'for safety' as he put it and we scrambled down the path back to the army base.

We were lucky, a lorry was just leaving for the 'Cotton Tree' which is a conspicuous landmark right in the centre of town. It is an enormous tree, several hundred years old and the natives have a saying, 'When there is no Cotton Tree, there will be no Freetown'. Time will tell.

We knew that from the Cotton Tree we could pick up a naval truck to Aberdeen and we clambered aboard over the back of the lorry to find a seat amongst a working party of native squaddies, all carrying machetes with which to hack down the bush wherever the sergeant pointed.

Bugsie was more than cheerful, he was exuberant and was soon laughing and joking with the lance-corporal on his right and, of course, the inevitable happened, Bugsie could contain his pride no longer and felt he had to share his joy with his new found friend. He put his hand inside his shirt and pulled out the black mamba and thrust it under the lance-corporal's nose. 'How about that?' he cried.

Pandemonium

If Bugsie had expected a reaction to his prize possession, he must have been more than gratified. West Africans know all there is to know about black mambas and none of it is good news. With a scream of terror the soldier raised his machete above his head and I just managed to grab his arm before we found out whether he was aiming at Bugsie or the snake.

Pandemonium reigned. I fell in a heap on the floor with our machete-wielding friend, while the rest of the troops scrambled to the far end behind the driver's cab in an attempt to put as much distance between themselves and the mamba and all of them banging like crazy on the driver's window yelling for him to stop, which he did with alacrity, throwing everyone in a heap on the floor on top of me and the corporal.

A white sergeant came running round the back to see what all the commotion was about and everyone started talking at once and pointing to Bugsie and the snake.

'It's dead', said Bugsie.

'Out', said the sergeant and in no time at all the lorry was disappearing towards town sans two matelots.

We walked the remaining couple of miles to the Cotton Tree and caught our truck back to camp and with great self-control, Bugsie obeyed my instructions and 'kept his bloody snake inside his shirt!'

Next day he lovingly skinned it and sent the skin home in a Privilege Envelope. I often wonder what his mother made of that!

Pressure

It was at this time that we had our first serious casualty. We were all under a lot of pressure and had been living in pretty poor conditions and most of us had been out there for too long and we all coped with it in various ways according to our different natures. Some drank to excess, a small minority took to the brothels and finished up wishing they hadn't. Which invited us to paraphrase the popular song 'whenever I piss I worry and wonder' amid loud guffawas of laughter from all except the poor wretch who had 'caught the boat up'.

My personal remedy was to play soccer or swim or run until I was exhausted. I neded a woman like crazy but at the risk of sounding sanctimonious, I thanked my lucky stars for my Boys' Brigade training, for although my moral standards were light years below that of the innocent sixteen year old of yesteryear, it still had enough hold on me to stop me sinking without a trace.

But to return to those who fell by the wayside, Ginger Bates was a robust likeable character, a good footballer and always ready for a laugh, but the insiduous rottenness of life in the White Man's Grave finally wore him down.

Mental Breakdown

The first signs were his regular bouts of drinking in the mess. We all drank pretty heavily but the shrewd ones had a break in between, those who didn't were on a collision course with disaster. Unfortunately, Ginger had a mild bout of malaria and when he came back from the general hospital and returned to his drinking habits the end came rapidly.

He was subjected to frequent fits of crying and eventually he had a complete mental breakdown and was sent home a gibbering wreck.

Nobody laughed at him in his misery, we knew that there but for the grace of God, go I. . .

Twenty-One Today

Suddenly one fine day Benny announced, 'I'm 21 today. Come and have a drink on me in the canteen tonight.' We had a terrific time, the beer flowed and we sang ourselves hoarse. The lower deck had a rather crude method of providing entertainment. They went round the entire gathering with the chant, 'We call on old (whoever) to sing us a song, sing y'bastard sing! Sing, sing or show us your ring!'

As anything was likely to happen once you dropped your trousers, nine out of ten chose to sing. It was a sure fire recipe for a lively evening and the success of Benny's birthday party was assured. Two days later Fred announced his twenty-first birthday and the format was repeated. Within a week Toddy became of age, then Gus-Gus, then me and Bugsie.

We should have seen it coming for we all registered under the same age group. I have only the haziest recollection of my twenty-first birthday party. I can remember a table covered in the inevitable Black Horse beer bottles and tripping over my guests lying in the gutter as I staggered out of the mess.

Doodle-Bugs and Rockets

As for the key of the door, the doodlebugs (or flying bombs, if you prefer) were dropping thick and fast on London and my family were still facing up to the Boche while me (your actual hero) was evacuated to West Africa. I would be lucky if there was a front door left to put a key into.

D-Day

'Crack of doom' was at it again with fantastic stories of the doodlbugs. Apparently they were incredibly accurate and were selecting special targets at Hitler's commands. Hackney marshes was the number one target as there was a lot of secret work going on there.

If you thought about it, anything that chugs along till it conks out and then falls out of the sky can hardly be described as having pinpoint accuracy, but like most rumours there was a certain amount of truth in what he said. In fact the V1s that fell on hackney marshes found that the horse had already bolted for the marshes had been used to build the Mulberry Harbour for the D-Day landings and at long last we had opened the Second Front.

By the time the first doodlebugs were launched, Mulberry was already securely in place on the Normandy beaches.

Our prophet of doom lived near the West Ham football stadium and told a confused story of the invasion troops being locked in there and running out of beer, so they broke out and went round the local pubs. By so doing they could have alerted any fifth column agent to the fact that the moment of truth had arrived, but despite this and in spite of people like Jack Boom shooting their mouths off, the invasion was as near a surprise to the Germans as an operation of this size could hope to be.

D-Day! Wouldn't I have loved to be aboard a battle wagon off the coast of Normandy pumping fifteen inch shells into the German defenses!

'Or scrambling out of a landing craft, clutching a rifle

and trying in vain to reach those same German defences at the top of the beach, while a murderous crossfire of machine guns mowed us down like ninepins?' I asked myself.

Heroes can't just choose to pose on the bridge of a battleship, they go willingly into suicidal situations and lay down their lives if necessary.

I thought of our recent twenty-first birthday parties and how full of life we all were and for the first time in the war I didn't feel bitter about missing out on the action.

Later my father wrote to say the good news was that the flying bombs (known as the V Ones) had almost stopped. The bad news was that a new bomb (known as the V Two) had taken its place. This, of course, was the first rocket ever to be used and on which Hitler banked his last hopes of winning the war. Thanks to the implacable courage of the British working classes, he drew a blank but he certainly embarrassed the would-be heroes sitting out the war in Sierra Leone.

Back to Print

For some time now I had been visiting the Government press where I introduced myself as a compositor's apprentice from London and asked if I could keep my hand in. There was a Scots Engineer who used to look after the linotype machines and he willingly let me try my hand (for we had no linotype machines at my tiny printshop in Edmonton) and eventually coached me to a moderate standard which I figured would give me a flying start in civvy street.

At the same time the governor who was a West African asked me to write a column on my immediate reactions to Sierra Leone. I had always wanted to be a journalist — indeed one of the first serious disagreements I had with my father was which path to choose, compositor or journalist, and as he already had an apprenticeship lined up for me, which he said represented security as opposed to the rat race of the editorial, I became a compositor.

With hindsight he was right for eventually as a piece case compositor in Fleet Street, I was earning more money than the sub-editors, but that's another story.

The Good News — And the Good News

The stories from the real war were suddenly becoming much better from the Allies' point of view. In July 1944 Tojo and his entire cabinet resigned — the first positive signs that the Japs were beginning to crack and in August the Russians captured Bucharest and the Rumanians wished they'd never joined.

September saw Antwerp recaptured more or less undamaged and the only hiccup was the severe mauling our magnificent airborne troops received at Arnhem. Most of this news was 'old hat' by the time it reached us and, of course, once it had been sub-edited by the propaganda department, even Arnhem sounded good.

Meanwhile I jumped at the chance to write for the Sierra Leone Weekly News and poured my heart out to my waiting readers (I still have my first copy at home), and the Editor was well pleased and my wages were a slap up feed in a Freetown restaurant.

The Card School

My editorial career was shortlived because of an unfortunate development and as usual the fly in the ointment was the Chief. Twice a week when our watches made it convenient we had a heavy card school in a quiet corner of the mess, and always in the forefront was John Holmes, a lad from Birmingham who sported a magnificent black beard and whose appetite for gambling was insatiable. His one objective since he arrived was to bankrupt me and take over all my operations — in the nicest possible way of course.

We had just finished a solo school and had started a game of pontoon and the table was littered with money. It was my bank and I was nonchalently flipping the cards across to the punters when round the corner came the Chief and within two strides had reached the table. He knew exactly what he was looking for and had obviously been tipped off.

'Bang to Rights'

Unfortunately I had my back to him and while the other three were able to scoop their money off the table and throw their hands into the middle, by the time I heard the word 'Chief', his hand was already on top of my money.

'That'll do nicely, Windsor', he said. 'I think I've got you bang to rights. I'm not sure I can prove anything against the rest of you, unless your mate here wants to give evidence against you. Would you like to co-operate, Windsor?' he asked.

'Get lost', I snarled. But the Chief was feeling too full of himself to take offence.

'Report for defaulters at 0900', he snapped and strode smartly away taking four pounds two shillings and sixpence of my money with him.

I caught him up as he stepped outside the mess and suggested we had a talk. 'All right, talk', he said.

'I have in my possession a football coupon signed G. Stevenson', I said. 'The skipper might think you've got double standards if I produced that'.

He called my bluff. 'I knew it was you behind that coupon', he replied. 'Well you'll find my signature is printed in capital letters, so you won't prove much with that, and furthermore if you do produce it tomorrow you'll go down for ninety days for sure'.

I was sunk without a trace and we both knew it.

Next morning I was up in front of the skipper and pleading my case that we'd been out here for our alloted span with virtually no entertainment and this was just our way of spending our spare time.

I have a feeling the CO was none too pleased with the Chief making unnecessary waves, but rules are rules and I'd broken them and he had to go by the book. He confiscated my four pounds two shillings and sixpence, which laughingly went into the entertainment fund and sent me to the detention centre in the main naval barracks for fourteen days.

The camp was shocked that I got fourteen days just for a game of cards, for most of them had a game at some time or another. It was the obvious way of passing the time and the Chief's popularity sunk even lower if that were possible. A small crowd came to see me off on what should have been the 'liberty lorry' and the Chief came out of his office to gloat but the booing became so loud and pointed that he went back in again.

The Detention Centre

On arrival at the detention centre I was put in a hut with nineteen other men and there were two more huts containing a similar number, one on either side of us. 'I never realised so many people got caught playing cards',

I joked to the chap in the next bunk. 'You could fill a book with what this lot's been up to', he grinned.

We soon realised that apart from the drill which was a pain in the neck or wherever, that there was never a dull moment for the men under punishment. It became obvious that there was a shortage of men in the main naval barracks (perhaps they'd even been sent to the war) and whenever they couldn't find anyone at short notice, they rooted out the men under punishment.

At first our chores were pretty elementary, such as patrolling the inside of the perimeter fence with a sturdy baton in our hand. You may think that this was to stop the inmates going AWOL, but you would be way off the mark. The reason we were there was to stop the natives from creeping under the barbed wire and nicking everything they could get their thieving hands on.

A Tap on the Head

Our instructions were explicit — 'Tap 'em on the head with your baton (you can't hurt 'em) and then push them back under the fence.' I did this patrol on several occasions and never tired of following those instructions. I'm sure the brass hat who suggested there was a Field Marshal's baton in every man's haversack never quite had us in mind when he said it.

I soon graduated from there to the brothel patrol in Freetown. They selected half a dozen of us who weren't already inside for fighting the police in brothels and we were taken to the Cotton Tree where we reported to a young lieutenant who looked still wet behind the ears. However, he wasn't wet enough to stick his neck out and pointing to me he said, 'I have some paperwork to do, so you take the patrol round this area which is about a quarter of a mile square and report back to me in an hour with any prisoners. Carry on', and he disappeared into one of the more select bars.

Houses of Ill Repute

I was in my element for some of the streets on my beat you would be crazy to venture into on your own at night, but with a naval patrol behind me I couldn't care less who was down there, although two of my squad were obviously not the sort that relished a punch-up and protested furiously when we entered the most notorious street in the area, but they had no choice but to follow or they would have been left on their own like babes in the wood.

We had a ball for the next hour as we entered houses of ill repute, making enough noise to wake the dead — for we had no intention of catching anyone. We swept the protesting 'ladies' aside and watched legs and behinds disappearing out of the back windows. In their haste they frequently lert half empty beer bottles which we confiscated as part of the job.

The whole operation seemed pretty pointless to me and we made about as much impact as King Canute had on the tide, for as fast as we moved from one street to the next, the clients came flooding back to reclaim their belongings and anything else they had paid for and not received, but as far as I was concerned it was an exciting and educational evening and miles better than languishing in the nick.

A Gay Time

Back at the detention centre the bunk on my left hand side was occupied by a nice lad who was obviously inside for being too nice to everyone. On the first night I was awakened to find him clambering under my mosquito net. I grabbed him by the ears and heaved him straight through the other side and he landed in a heap on the floor and his yells of distress woke up the whole hut.

They say that after ninety days at sea sodomy is legal, although I suspect that was a 'fairy' tale concocted by some dirty old three badger as a means of seducing young seamen. At any rate it wasn't a very popular pastime among the vast majority of the ratings I met, and we were all getting fed up with this amorous misfit. When he wasn't pestering one of us he would slip out after lights out and visit a stoker-diver in the next hut and eventually our patience and tolerance exhausted, we arranged a reception committee for him.

As he crept back in the wee small hours, we grabbed him and tipped him head first into a huge static water tank at the rear of the hut. To stop the mosquitos from breeding the water was covered with a film of oil and as our perverted comrade clambered out with oil streaming down his hair and face he sobbed, 'I can't help it if I can't control my passion!'

I almost felt sorry for him.

Boarding Party

The next night we had barely got off to sleep when the Chief (not my old adversary at Aberdeen) switched on the lights and came round banging his baton on the bunks and creating a fearful racket.

'Men under punishment fall in', he yelled. We stood there, most of us without a stitch on, wondering if the end of the world was at hand and he walked purposely down the line and handed out a dozen batons (yes, of course I got one) and then he said, 'You lot get your number threes on and muster outside in five minutes. The rest of you dismiss'.

Speculation was rife. Surely they weren't dragging us out on a brothel patrol at this time of night? We marched down to the quay where a cutter was waiting and on the command we piled aboard and the Chief at last offered us an explanation.

'You're going to capture the enemy', he cried.

I could scarcely contain myself as I thought of the Bismark or the Scharnhorst.

'What in this?' I asked him.

'Yes, in this very boat', he replied. 'What do you think of that?' There were plenty of responses that showed what the majority thought of that — not bloody much! However, we chugged out into the night wondering if we'd been cast adrift with a nut case, when we began to make out two dark shapes in the harbour. The first was a frigate from the Freetown Escort and the second was a merchant ship just heaving to.

Not only was she considerably less formidable than the Bismark but she was flying the Spanish flag!

'That's the enemy?' I asked incredulously.

'You'd better believe it' said the Chief, 'that little beauty has been supplying the U-boats at sea!'

Just in Case

It occurred to me that we weren't going to be terribly welcome aboard this dirty hulk of Spanish merchandise and my baton which had seemed all powerful patrolling the camp perimeter, suddenly seemed rather puny facing the unknown. I glanced at the Chief's belt and noted he had a gun in it (I'm all right, Jack) and seeing the object of my attention he patted it and said, 'Just in case'.

'In case of what?' I thought. With hindsight, we probably had the punchlines for a TV commercial.

By now we were alongside the discredited merchant ship. The rails were lined by nine or ten sullen looking seamen, utterly scruffy and looking utterly evil. The 64,000 dollar question was how evil were they and did they think the Nazi cause was worth dying for. Well we'd soon know.

The chief stood up in the cutter and with his revolver in his hand made a motion that he wanted a rope thrown down and after a couple of minutes bobbing up and down on the considerable swell, there was a thump and down it came. This was already a major victory.

'Make Fast Aft'

At this moment I realised I had made a tactical error by sitting in the stern, for without a moment's hesitation, the Chief flung the end of the rope at me and shouted 'Make fast aft.' Now with modest pride I can say I was a pretty good telegraphist, but seaman? That was something else! Managing to put my back between me and the Chief I twisted the rope two or three times round the appropriate place and tied two dirty great knots in it for good measure, called out 'made fast, Chief', and swarmed up the iron ladder that ran down the side of the ship.

My crewmates were impressed that I was so keen to be the first to enter the fray, without realising I was merely making a diversionary manoeuvre to take the Chief's mind off the rope. It seemed the lesser of two evils. Reluctantly the crew stood to one side to let us board. They looked menacing enough but 'discretion is the better part of valour', and seeing as they were shanghaied in a British port with a frigate's guns trained on them at point blank range, they were on mission impossible.

Franco Repays a Debt

By now General Franco must have realised that he was backing a loser for the Second Front had already started, but he still had a debt to repay to the Fascist Dictators for without their help he would never have taken Spain and now with the U-boats unable to use their French bases, Hitler had called in his chips and with fear and trepidation Spanish merchant ships were keeping the U-boats at sea.

Not that the crews of the U-boats felt terribly grateful for their help, for during 1943 and 1944 their losses had been horrific and the bonus of extra weeks at sea, thanks to Franco, did not compare with the alternative of being tucked up in bed with a fraulein.

So here I was, nearly a hero again. I'd mixed it with voodoo men, Italian prisoners of war and now Spanish merchantmen — and they call this a war?

Hold the Ship

The Chief called 'fall in' and explained the position. We were to hold the ship until the morning watch when a crew from the main barracks would take over. Meanwhile he divided us into pairs and sent us in different directions to scour the ship and make sure they were not up to any funny business.

None of us found any 'funny business'. There was no ammunition and not too much food and it was clear that we had locked the stable door after the horse had bolted. She had obviously supplied her U-boats and was on her way home when she had been intercepted. The Chief said later that they had found documentary evidence to this effect, which was just as well or there would have been egg on somebody's face.

The only funny thing I noticed was half a dozen live sheep in the hold and I wondered how they had coped with being tossed up and down in the Atlantic. It couldn't have been much fun when you've been used to a flat meadow all your life.

Perhaps they had been destined for the last U-boat and their transfer had been interrupted by the frigate's untimely appearance on the horizon. I could well imagine the panic stations that would have caused.

The rating I was coupled up with was a ferocious-looking Yorkshireman whose hobby was GBH and if he couldn't find a punch-up he would start one. Part of our territory included the galley and in no time at all 'GBH' had unearthed a crate of wine and without further ado began drinking out of a bottle. The Chief was up on the bridge interrogating the skipper and as he was a typical Englishman abroad (if they don't understand, you shout louder) it was obviously going to take some time for either of them to get any sense out of the other, so I quietly contacted six of our squad and invited them in for a drink.

We had to show our faces every now and then through the night, just to let the Chief know we were still with him and every now and then we nipped back to the galley for a noggin, but eventually GBH tired of putting in an appearance and pitched camp beside his crate of wine.

One Adrift

He was still there when the relief boarding party arrived led by a sublieutenant. After congratulating the

Chief on doing a grand job, they both realised that we were one man adrift and detailed one of the lieutenant's party to fetch him.

I winced at the thought and sure enough the rating was back in one minute flat nursing a bloody nose and requesting help. The young lieutenant snorted and telling his men to follow, he plunged below deck. We could hear the resulting fracas from where we stood and eventually a somewhat bedraggled officer appeared, followed by two ratings half dragging a struggling GBH up on deck.

Apparently the sublieutenant had the effrontary to snatch the bottle from the drunken Yorkshireman's hand and demand that he stand up. In the melée that followed the sub got a punch in the eye and GBH got a tap over the head with a baton as the only means of controlling him.

One Last Chore

It was time to say farewell to our prize ship and the Chief was already standing in the cutter waiting for Yorkie to be bundled in. As an afterthought he realised that his own baton was still aboard the ship and that he might well need it in the next thirty seconds, so he shouted to me, 'Let me have your baton'. There was a considerable swell running by now and at the moment of his request he was only about eight feet below me, so with my usual enthusiasm I shouted 'catch', and threw it straight at him. If only I'd been a seaman I would have realised that a swell goes up and down and by the time my baton reached him he was at least twenty feet below me in a trough, with the result that it flew straight over his head and floated swiftly out of sight.

The Chief was gibbering with rage but the arrival of

the prisoner (for that was now the status of GBH) diverted his attention from me and we all piled aboard.

Another thought occurred to me that I might soon be in the limelight again as I deliberately made my way forward. 'Cast off aft' called the Chief and there was feverish activity round the rope accompanied by muffled curses. 'I said cast off aft', shouted the Chief.

'Can't get the bloody thing undone' came the reply and the Chief pushed his way through to investigate.

'What stupid sod tied this?' he demanded. 'Me, Chief', I confessed.

'Don't you know anything?' he screamed, obviously still uptight about the baton.

'Well, I'm a sparks', I said, 'sparks don't tie knots'.

'I'd like to tie a knot round your bloody neck' he snorted as we eventually cast off and made our way back to base.

This should have been the end of this episode as far as I was concerned, but the men under punishment had one more chore to perform before our sentence was up. We were required to escort Yorkie to his court martial. We waited patiently outside while GBH was tried by a full commander who duly found him guilty and sentenced him to ninety days, at which GBH went berserk and leapt over the desk and grabbed the commander by the throat. We last saw him being dragged off to the cells and I reckon they probably threw away the key.

In case you haven't figured it out, GBH stands for Grievous Bodily Harm.

The One That Got Away

While I was doing my time fate struck a particularly cruel blow which actually made my punishment really hurt, for in truth my time at the detention centre had been so different from the monotony of watchkeeping that I'd almost enjoyed it, but now came the crunch.

The day I'd gone to the detention centre a cruiser no less, had called in at Freetown and needed a few hands to make up her complement and of all things had requested a special operator! This time there was no short list, the skipper had picked one of the longest serving members of the ship's company for two reasons: (a) because they were more experienced, and (b) because they should have been on their way home any way. In the event a lad named Dutton got the job and as he was noted for speaking up when he felt the situation warrented, and was also one of the Chief's pet hates, I felt I had all the credentials to have had at least a fifty fifty chance of selection.

After the war someone said they had heard a rumour that Dutton had been lost at sea. In any event we never saw him again, but that neither proved or disproved anything.

Shark!

I reported back to the Chief's office and he came out for a little 'gloat', but it was obvious even to him that I had not had half as bad a time as he had hoped and that I was pretty full of myself.

A mate from the welcoming committee called out, 'How was it, Dave?' to which I replied truthfully, 'A bloody sight better than here!' which really made the Chief's day.

After lunch I went down to the beach with Bugsie and we could see in the distance a crowd of excited villagers on the beach and a small fishing boat just off the shore. We hurried to the spot and saw about a dozen men dragging a huge net onto the shore and from the trepidation on their faces they had obviously got something pretty big and pretty fierce inside it.

As we drew near we could see it was a shark of immense proportions, and it was thrashing about and snapping wildly at its tormentors, although the enormous net was obviously cramping its style.

Not a Pretty Sight

Finally they got it clear of the water and dumped it a few yards up the beach where they threw the entire net around it and clubbed it to death. It was not a pretty sight and we winced as the creature's head was slowly battered to pulp, but the crowd, women and children included, laughed and clapped as their menfolk did the deed, for this to them was the old enemy and they were taking sweet revenge for many of their kinsmen who had died an equally terrible death by the jawas of these sea monsters.

If we thought that this was revolting, the best had yet to come, for no sooner was it dead than they slit the shark open from top to bottom, and the entire crowd took it in turns to dip their hands into its entrails and crammed its raw intestines into their mouths.

Enough was enough, we left hurriedly feeling distinctly queasy, but as Bugsie explained afterwards, 'It's just what you are used to'.

Me? I'll stick to eggs and bacon.

Iron Crosses Galore

As far as the war was concerned I had completely missed the boat. 'D Day' had come and gone and the Second Front was rolling steadily along, although the

Germans were resisting fiercely every inch of the way to Berlin. It struck me as ironic that they were now in exactly the same position as we were in 1940 when we stood alone against the rest of Europe with even Russia signing pacts and giving sustenance to the Nazis.

Their only surviving ally had more than enough problems in the Far East to be of any help to them, but just as we had done when all seemed lost, they soldiered on. I thought of all those Iron Crosses that were up for grabs and realised that I must be growing up, for I didn't envy them one little bit.

However, I was pretty browned off by now and would welcome any opportunity to get out of the rut. The opportunity presented itself the following day when I was in charge of the supply lorry to Kissi Barracks (yes, again).

While they were loading I met an 'Oppo' of mine who had considerable influence in the draft chit section. He knew I was a printer in civvy street and told me that they needed someone in the main barracks to run the one man printshop as the previous printer had finished his time.

My Kingdom for a Ship

I was tempted to make the change if it could be fiddled but once again my dream interferred. You can't win a war in a print shop!

'What I want is a ship', I stated categorically, 'and it's worth four tins of tickler (a small fortune in tobacco) if you can get me one'.

'Let us see', said my fellow conspirator, 'you're a sparks, so that shouldn't be difficult. I'm pretty sure one of the Freetown Escort want one. Do you fancy it?'

Did I fancy it!

Within ten minutes I had a draft chit for a ship of my own and he had my promissary note for four tins of tickler. I still didn't hold out much hope for my chances, but fate was definitely on my side. The Chief who would have squashed it flat, was away for a couple of days and Mac our killick was 'acting Petty Officer'.

He didn't like it one bit, but the chitty was legal and for old times sake he agreed to let me scarper without reporting it immediately to the duty officer who was busy trying to convince a lady friend that she was sex starved and would cheerfully have let me desert to the Germans rather than put his trousers back on.

The Imposter

In eight minutes exactly I had stuffed all my gear into a kitbag and given Bugsie everything I couldn't manage and was back on the same lorry heading for the barracks en route for the high seas. The next day another lorry dumped me alongside a sleek blue-grey River Class frigate and I boarded my very first warship with a considerable amount of fear and trepidation.

The fear was not of Admiral Donnitz and his merry men, but a very real obstacle to my fulfilling my mission — I simply wasn't qualified for the job.

The drafting office had assumed (as I hoped they would) that a telegraphist S.O. was the same as any other telegraphist, whereas we were poles apart and I knew my first couple of weeks were going to be difficult in the extreme.

Unfortunately HMS Ware (which is as near as I propose to get to naming her) was in for a minor refit and for nearly a week I was looking over my shoulder in case a press gang turned up from Aberdeen to reclaim an escaped Special Operator. It seemed quite perverse to have a press gang dragging sailors off ships instead of the other way round, but my fears proved completely unfounded for they either hadn't missed me (which meant the duty officer had scored) or they didn't know where to look.

There were a million questions I wanted to ask but I knew if I asked them before we put to sea the game would be up, so I contented myself with keeping my eyes and ears ever on the alert and gleaned just enough knowledge to make it seem that I was the genuine article. I figured that once we set sail I would have at least two weeks to become part of the set up, and once I'd proved I could do it, they would accept me.

But the best laid plans of mice and men. . .

In that time I made several good friends and had a couple of runs 'ashore'. 'Ashore!' I had never been anywhere else for the past two years.

To Sea at Last

Came the great day and we cast off heading towards Gibraltar to meet a convoy of merchant ships, mostly carrying supplies for the West African forces and a few troops to replace those who had served their time. For apart from the U-boats the war had by-passed West Africa and most of the action was in Germany and the Far East. The Russians had pretty well cleared the Boche from their beloved land and the siege of Leningrad had ended after almost nine hundred days with the besieging Germans surrendering. It was estimated that a million people died in Leningrad and after the war Stalin named it 'Heroes City', but now the Russians with revenge in their hearts were sweeping westward towards Berlin.

Meanwhile my heart soared as we steamed into the South Atlantic but my troubles were mounting in the wireless room as it became apparent that I didn't know the procedures, call signs or anything else that wasn't to do with U-boats.

The Leading Telegraphist took it pretty well, but was not too happy at the thought of standing his watch and mine. The second day out I was learning fast but still had a long way to go — you can't master six months of training in two days — when much as a boxer trapped against the ropes is saved by the bell, we developed engine trouble and had to turn back to Freetown.

Home is the Hero

Within three days of setting sail under the White Ensign I was back in port and in the nicest possible way the Chief had bundled me aboard a lorry heading back to HMS Aberdeen with the words 'Bloody Imposter' ringing in my ears.

Inevitably Chief Stevenson was waiting to welcome me back aboard with the threat that I would pay for this little escapade — and that's a promise!

My old bunk was still empty in the hut and within ten minutes it was just as though I'd never been away.

Molly

Now came the incident which transformed my last few months in Sierra Leone from the deepest gloom to a pinacle of ecstacy and it came in the shape of a buxom lass with a winning smile and the simple name of 'Molly'. She was not a raving beauty but she simply oozed sex appeal and had such a likeable personality that I was completely bowled over.

It didn't take a detective to establish that she worked at the hospital for she was still wearing her nurse's uniform and I watched her from the other side of the road, much as Adam must have looked at Eve, for it was an accepted fact of life that the nurses only went out with officers and she was the forbidden fruit.

She stood under the Cotton Tree looking cool and composed although from the pallor of her skin and the newness of her uniform she had obviously arrived only recently. She was gently swinging her handbag (another sure sign of inexperience) when the inevitable happened. From behind the tree and also behind the unsuspecting nurse strolled a burly teenager and when he was within two paces of her, he sprang forward and with the skill of an expert barged her in the back and snatched the handbag in one swift movement.

As she fell to the ground he sprinted towards a narrow street across the square and that was his first mistake, for I was slightly nearer the entrance than he was. He was still glancing over his shoulder to see if there was a hue and cry when I hurled myself forward in a rugby tackle, and fetched him crashing to the ground. I was first on my feet and my solid naval boot dealt him a sharp kick in the vitals which I would imagine precluded his sex life for the next month or so and I snatched the bag from his feeble fingers, leaving him groaning in the gutter and walked briskly back to the nurse who was just rising to her feet.

Farmer's Daughter

She couldn't thank me enough and while modesty is not my long suit I began to blush with embarrassment at the hero worship. Me, who had been trying to become a hero since 1939!

I suggested that we went into the nearest bar while she recovered and over the drinks we swapped information about ourselves. Her father had a farm in Suffolk and for a time she'd been in the Women's Land Army but she felt she needed a change and after a short period as a trainee nurse she had volunteered for overseas, which was my good luck for here I was chatting up my first girl for two years. I had a feeling that she hadn't told me the whole story, but that would keep.

She rose from the table, saying she had to get back on duty and gave me a lingering kiss just to say 'Thank you' and I felt a stirring in my loins, which after all this time wasn't surprising. She obviously felt it too for she gave me a knowing smile, so I plucked up my courage and hoping against hope, asked if I could see her again. I was amazed when she agreed, for she could have had fifty better offers from the upper classes, but she readily agreed to meet me under the Cotton Tree in three days time and crossed the square to catch a Bedford van that was going back to the hospital.

A brief wave from the window and she was gone and I went back to the bar to await the lorry back to camp.

My Canoe

The intervening days until we met again should have seemed an eternity but there was always something to break the monotony, especially with Gus around always hovering in the wings. I had recently bought a canoe from one of the lads in the village for the bargain price of a tin of fifty cigarettes. It was moored in the mangrove swamp and we had been practicing with the thing and found it was nowhere as easy as the natives made it look. Its centre of balance was not in the centre of the boat, so we had an hilarious time watching each other get in one side and fall out the other, but at long last we had managed to stay put and paddle around the swamp.

Of course Gus had to push his luck and boasted that on a calm day he and I (well, it was my canoe) could take it out to sea. Benny who could always be wound up by Gus, promptly pulled a 'Reddy' (West African pound notes were red, hence the expression) out of his pocket and grated, 'that says you can't take it round the point'. Gus promptly covered it and said, 'We'll see you in the cove this afternoon'.

I should explain the geography of the course which Benny had set. First we carried the boat from the mangrove swamp to the beach and then paddled round the point which marked the entrance to the bay and had a small red and white lighthouse to guide the convoys in.

Side Bets

Just round the point was a small deep cove which was ideal for swimming and diving — with the usual proviso, watch out for the baracudas — and we were to paddle into the cove and carry the canoe overland back to the swamp. There was a further side bet of another pound that we couldn't do it in under two hours. Gus wasn't particularly a betting man so to give me an incentive to go with him (and presumably lend him my canoe) he let me have a half share of his bet, which was ten shillings we wouldn't make the cove and ten shillings we wouldn't be back in the swamp by 1400 hours. It was agreed Bugsie would draw our tots at noon and meet us at the finishing line.

Usually I am quietly confident when on a betting

mission, but this was not my idea and I had an albatros round my neck in the shape of Gus who was a born loser. Anyway, at eight bells we picked up the canoe and with some misgivings I trotted behind Gus to the beach. He waded out until the water was waist deep and with his usual enthusiasm Mr 200% leapt into the boat, turning it upside down and disappeared beneath the foam.

This much was par for the course and didn't upset or surprise me, indeed I would have been positively amazed if we had got straight into the canoe and paddled sedately for the point. I hoped that this would get him to simmer down and we could get on with it, but Gus was already demonstrating his panache for doing things the hard way and was leaping up and down with the tentacles of a Portuguese man of war wrapped round his leg. We freed him with the aid of a paddle and he gingerly climbed aboard rubbing his leg which must have been quite sore and then even more gingerly we struck out for the open sea heading round the point.

'The Andes'

After some ten minutes we had established a rhythm and our balance was pretty well co-ordinated and we felt we had every chance of beating the deadline. In just over an hour we were rounding the point about a quarter of a mile out to sea to be well clear of the rocks and the currents that swirled round them and we turned into the bay with a feeling of mild elation — but I had reckoned without the Albatros.

One of the most welcome sights in Freetown was the Dutch liner the 'Andes' which regularly fetched troops and, more importantly, mail into the port. She was a magnificent ship of considerable tonnage and I was always stirred by the sight of her. I was about to be deeply moved by the sight of her in an unforgettable close-up for as we straightened up to enter the bay she was just leaving harbour and was apparently heading stright for us.

I now know the true meaning of 'Panic Stations' for we both spotted her together. I tried to paddle like mad towards the cove, while Gus went into reverse to go back round the point. In the event we wallowed for several minutes while the Andes towered past us looking like a mobile Empire State Building.

It probably missed us by a hundred yards, but the wash was tremendous. It picked us up like a piece of driftwood and fortunately hurled us in the direction of the cove. We came through the entrance as though we were jet propelled, and we were both tossed out as the canoe overturned losing our paddles, but we managed to cling on to the canoe and kicked out towards the landing stage. I was pretty well exhausted and had swallowed a considerable amount of sea water, and Gus was 'all in' as his swimming was still not in the super bracket and he was coughing and spluttering something alarming.

'Tantamount to Cheating'

Benny and Toddy, who were already waiting at the cove to see the outcome of the wager, realised the situation and stripped off and swam out to help us, which was just as well for in our weakened state there was a very real danger that we would be swept out of the cove again with the backwash and out into the bay.

They dragged us onto the landing stage and we lay there for a full five minutes, spluttering and retching, when Gus, who had made a remarkable recovery said in a triumphant voice, 'Come on, Dave, we've got half an hour to get back to the swamp'.

Benny went bananas. 'And what do you think that's going to get you?' he demanded.

'Well, our two quid for a start', said Gus.

'Two quid!' exploded Banny. 'You wouldn't be bloody alive, let alone have a boat to carry back, if it wasn't for me and Toddy!'

'Well that's tantamount to cheating', said Gus. 'We had right of way, everybody knows that steam must give way to sail and if the Andes skipper had been more experienced, he would have gone round us. I say you're welching on the bet'.

I winced as I heard Gus pushing his luck and watched as Benny with a bellow of rage, picked him up and tossed Gus off the quayside. 'And this time rescue your bloody self', he roared.

Back at the swamp we tied up my canoe — sans paddles — and sat in a sodden circle while Bugsie dispensed the rum rations and by mutual consent all bets were off.

A Date with a Dream

Came the great day and I was dressed far smarter than I had ever been on Trafalgar Day Parade. Obviously I didn't fancy Nelson half as much as Molly. I disembarked from the liberty lorry and stood anxiously in the cool shade of the Cotton Tree for although it was only 0930 hours, it was already hot enough for an English summer's day and it would be well over one hundred degrees by noon.

By 0940 she was already ten minutes late and I was beginning to curse myself for being an over-optimistic fool when, lo and behold, the Bedford van arrived in the square and there she was alighting from it! She started to cross towards me and her smile was radiant, but I couldn't wait for her to reach the Cotton Tree and hurried towards her, meeting her halfway across the main road. We met and I kissed her on both cheeks in true continental style (as instructed by Toddy who said he knew of these things) and she loved it, and gave me a hug, by which time a minor traffic jam had built up and the hooting and swearing rather spoilt the atmosphere. Who said all the world loves a lover?

We retired to the bar where we had first met and I deliberately picked the same table and we held hands and gazed into each other's eyes. If we weren't in love, we were perilously close to it.

The Pickpocket

As I suspected she was fairly new to Sierra Leone and had not seen much of Freetown and she asked me to show her around the district, which presented me with my first problem — where to take her, for the Freetown I knew was composed of dingy bars and punch-ups or the seaman's mission and none of the high class clubs were open to other ranks — not even to the ship's bookmaker who could afford to patronise them where many a sublieutenant could not.

We left the bar and strolled down the High Street, window shopping and then on to the market and here I almost blotted my copy book. Part of our tropical uniform consisted of a belt with a pouch at the front in which we kept our banknotes, a fact which was well known to the young urchins who had developed a technique of running past you from behind, flipping up the flap and snatching the notes without pausing in their stride.

Sublimely oblivious to the world around us, we must have seemed an easy target for the lad who was tailing us, and when he made his move he must have thought he was home and dry. He was unlucky in as much as I was an old hand out there and even when I was entirely captivated by Molly, I was subconsciously deeply aware that the market was a danger area and I had to be on my toes.

Consequently as soon as I felt him flip my pouch open, my fist crashed down on his fingers before he could remove the money and with a reflex action, my boot came up and caught him a painful kick up the rear which lifted him screaming into the air before he crashed to the ground.

Crash Course

Immediately I knew I had made a 'faux pas' for while my shipmates would have applauded my skill and dexterity and considered I had scored a major victory, I realised that Molly was a caring person who was probably horrified by violence, especially inflicted on a thirteen-year old youth. I tried to make amends by helping him to his feet, but I couldn't resist lecturing him at the same time for I particularly wanted Molly to know why I had done it, for she obviously had no idea what was going on. The lad brushed himself down and hobbled off and I apologised for over-reacting and explained there was a permanent war going on between the young pickpockets and the troops and that was the only punishment available as there was no chance of them being put in prison. To my intense relief she smiled and said she had obviously got a lot to learn about West Africa but I was certainly giving her a crash course.

We had lunch and another drink at a bar and then strolled down to the riverside skirting a shanty town which I suspected interested her far more than any plush night club could have done, and sure enough she took my arm and steered me towards the nearest shack.

She was not a high flier, just a simple country girl who wanted to see the real world for herself, and she was amazed at the conditions under which these people lived. Here I suspect was the first pangs of conscience which a decade later would open the flood gates of immigration to half the Third World.

Slumming

Unescorted she would not have dared to set foot in the slums of Freetown but she seemed confident that I could deal with any situation that could possibly arise and strolled earnestly amongst them, asking questions and offering sympathy. I was longing to tell her that the nice ones were just happy to talk, but if she didn't watch it the fly ones would con her for every last penny.

It was with some relief that I steered her away from the mud and corrugated iron shacks to the cleaner air down by the river.

'I'd like to rest for a while', she said wearily.

Sanctuary

I looked desperately round for a resting place but the river bank was an ochre coloured mud, baked hard by the tropical sun and I could imagine what that would do to her white skirt. A couple of hundred yards further on were three or four small boats moored to the bank. I had seen them there before and they seemed seldom used, so with the air of one who knows what he is doing, I took her arm and led her towards them.

Lady luck was with me for not only were they all unoccupied but the best of them, a neat little cabin cruiser clearly had its door very slightly open. I hauled it into the bank and we both hopped aboard, where-upon I played out the rope and we drifted twenty feet out into the river.

'There you are, madam', I cried, 'sanctuary'.

'Sanct you werry much', she laughed in her soft Suf-folk brogue which I was finding so entrancing. I loved the way she raised the pitch of her voice at the end of a sentence.

'Oh, Molly', I whispered and took her in my arms. My lips searched for hers and for several minutes we stood in a clinch with the world far away and my excitement growing with every second.

There was a very convenient double bunk in the cruiser and at the end of that passionate kiss, she slipped off her shoes and lay down with a contented sigh and motioned me to lie beside her.

Love at Last!

I needed no second bidding and pausing only to re-move my boots, I was with her on the bunk and clasping her to me. As gently as possible my hand reached for her bosom and meeting no opposition I slowly undid first one button and then another, until I had slipped off her blouse to reveal two beautifully formed breasts encased in a thirty six 'C' cup bra, although at that time the statistics meant nothing to me.

With fumbling fingers I groped round the back search-ing for the release mechanism and it was a great relief when she put one arm behind her back and with a deft movement, removed the impeding undergarment, and I gratefully sank my head into her bosom with a sigh of ecstacy. Soon I was nibbling her breasts and my right hand was exploring the rest of her gorgeous body. Clumsily but nevertheless gently, I removed her panties and felt my fingers softly caressing her silken thighs and stealing gently upwards.

She was moaning softly with delight and I felt her unbuttoning my shorts. It was a moment's work to remove them and she drew me to her.

Better and Better

I was more than ready for her but nevertheless I hesitated, I hadn't come prepared. Not in my wildest dreams did I imagine she would let me go this far, but we were madly in love, thousands of miles from home and there was a war on.

She read my thoughts. 'It's quite safe, darling', she whispered and I needed no second bidding. With a gasp of sheer delight, I was taking her.

I cannot pretend that I was the perfect lover at that moment for my sexual experience up to then was practically nil and in two minutes I could control myself no longer and it was over, but it is a memory I shall cherish for ever. She was so lovely, so sexy and so understanding.

'Don't worry, darling', she whispered, 'it will get better and better' and she was right. In just twenty minutes I was ready to perform again, and this time I could control my passion long enough to satisfy her.

She clung to me moaning with ecstacy as locked together, afire with desire, we finally reached the perfect climax and lay side by side, exhausted and blissfully happy.

'How could I ever find you in a hellhole like this, Molly?' I asked, caressing her tenderly.

She smiled that beautiful happy smile of hers, and answered, 'Don't you believe in fate, darling?'

Whirlwind of Love

I admitted that until this moment I had been a cynic and asked the question that had been bugging me. 'How did you know it would be safe?' I queried for I was not a true believer in sex by statistics.

Another smile and she replied, 'When I got drafted here the matron at home insisted that I had a dutch cap fitted — just in case. You were my 'just in case'.

'Just in case', I thought. 'Where have I heard that before?'

There was a small washroom aboard and after a shared ablution in that cosy and confined space we dressed and I went on deck and hauled us in to the bank. We reached the Cotton Tree in time for a quick drink before the Bedford arrived and after another passionate embrace she boarded it and blew me a kiss as it departed.

At last I knew the meaning of being on cloud nine.

For nearly two months we lived in a whirlwind of passionate love, both of us eagerly awaiting the next date when we could give ourselves to each other in our cabin cruiser, for we had now come to regard it as our own.

Even as we walked down the towpath towards the boat, my excitement was showing and she would give me a playful slap on my embarrassing bulge, then we would pause to hug and kiss before hurrying on to our love nest.

Once aboard we stripped off completely as a matter of routine and the mad desire that we aroused in each other took over completely. We were both twenty-one years of age, both extremely fit and both with an inexhaustable sex drive which complemented each other.

I began to wonder if we ever married how long we could keep this pace up, but hypothetical questions such as that were of no great importance — it would be great fun trying. Meanwhile the war was a million miles away and I had discovered that sex was a superb substitute, especially with a girl like Molly. I had to pinch myself to make sure I wasn't dreaming.

Doodlebugs and Rockets

I had to cancel our next date in order to sit my examination for Leading Telegraphist (S.O.) and it didn't help my concentration any to think of what I was missing, but I'd always been able to take exams in my stride and at the end of the day I felt pretty sure that I had passed. It wasn't that I particularly wanted a hook (it's the equivalent of a corporal in the other two services) but the war was going badly for Hitler. He had played all his trump cards as far as I could tell, his doodlebugs (flying bombs) and his rockets had created havoc in London without bringing the capital to its knees, for which I understand we are greatly indebted to Michel Hollard, an heroic member of the French Resistance who personally reconnoitred the V One sights and sent blueprints of them back to the RAF who struck at them with such devastating effect that the Germans had to abandon their original plan to despatch five thousand flying bombs a month to London and were reduced to about one sixth of that target which was still pretty devastating. Hollard saved London from obliteration but paid a terrible price, being captured and tortured by the Gestapo, but miraculously our hero survived the war.

Another trump card of Hitler's was the Battle of the Bulge which had so nearly given him a major victory but had now ended in disaster. All these things meant it was only a matter of time before the Russians, the Yanks and ourselves all met up in Berlin to celebrate Hitler's funeral, but it also meant that my demobilisation was not a million years away and when that happened the amount of redundancy pay you received would depend on your rank, hence the reason I swotted up for my hook.

My conscience was having a bad time over London. I'd left it with everyone slapping me on the back and wishing me luck, convinced that I was going to sock it to the Germans. A real hero's send-off and what happened? I'd been evacuated to Sierra Leone and the people who had cheered me off had been as much in the front line as at least three quarters of the servicemen had. I thought of my family at home, never knowing when the next rocket would fall from the sky without warning, yet carrying on as though nothing was happening to make sure that the troops had a home to come back to, and I knew who the real heroes were.

The Tabernacle

Another little gem from 'Crack of Doom', this time in praise of the V2. The rockets had been falling on London since the autumn of 1944 and they must have been particularly terrifying because of their silent approach. On the other hand, of course, you didn't know much about it.

Mr Boom sang the praises of this wonderful new invention (which indeed it was) but couldn't resist going over the top by claiming that at Hitler's command they could pinpoint individual buildings in London and for proof he maintained they had scored a direct hit on a tabernacle in Tottenham Court Road.

Toddy mildly suggested that if you sent over enough rockets on London one was eventually bound to hit a synagogue or tabernacle or whatever, but 'Crack of Doom' would have none of it. 'The Germans have entered the space age', he declared, 'and we can't cope with it'. This made us feel pretty good after five years of blood, sweat and tears to be told it was all in vain!

In the event the Allies coped with it by over-running their rocket launcher sites, but as usual Jack Boom's information was pretty accurate (I sometimes wondered whose side he was on) and a V2 had scored a direct hit on Whitfield Tabernacle in Tottenham Court Road, but the good news was that it was the last rocket to land on London for as I have said, contrary to Jack's claim, there was something we could do about it and by March 1945 they had destroyed the last launching pad and London could relax — at last!

F.D.R.

Some two weeks later President Franklin de Roosevelt died, and Britains everywhere mourned the passing of a true friend who had helped us in our darkest hour.

However, any amount of brooding on the state of things back home wouldn't change anything and from the examination room I made my way to the operations room to play war games with the U-boats.

Our Private Yacht

It was two more days before I met Molly again. She was already waiting at the Cotton Tree when I arrived and looking radiant in her white uniform. We ran to each other's arms and I hugged and hugged her, my cup of happiness was overflowing.

Over the drinks in the bar I told her about the exam and that I was hopeful and she asked, 'Does that mean you'll have another stripe to go with your present one?'

'Molly, dear', I explained, 'that little stripe has nothing to do with being a lance-corporal. It simply means that the navy has put up with me for three years. meanwhile I need you so badly that I will be of no further use to the navy until I've taken you aboard our private yacht and let you have your way with me.'

She stood up and gave a small curtsey. 'At your service, Captain', she smiled.

The sun blazed down and we were glad to enter the shady cabin with our familiar double bunk. Once more we helped each other with gentle movements and provocative touches that made us yearn for each other even before we laid down on the bunk, and then side by side our hands explored with subtle movements until we could stand it no longer ad we merged together in a frenzy of young passion.

'Oh, David, I do enjoy you so!' she purred, and my heart was full of contentment, for there is nothing more fulfilling than making love to a woman who really wants you.

The 64,000 Dollar Question

The exam results came and yours truly was one of the seven who had passed out of twelve entrants, and usually it was a formality for those successful to be sent to Kissi to be made up to leading hands, but this time there was a slight difference. One of the applicants had just come back from fourteen days in the detention centre and the 64,000 dollar question was 'Would the skipper recommend him?'

We waited all agog for the list to go up and to my delight and the Chief's chagrin, my name was included. It was obvious that the skipper thought I'd been punished enough for a game of cards and he was trying to tell the Chief something.

I managed to see my beloved Molly once more before the making up parade at Kissi and it was another divine experience. The whole afternoon was spent in wonderland with moments of ecstacy shared with exhausted rest periods while we fondled each other. Molly, darling, I can't bear to be away from you!

The Skate

Came the day to get my hook and there I was, dressed almost as smartly as if I was meeting Molly, standing in line outside the Commander's office. My heart sank when I saw the Chief in charge of the parade — it was my old adversary from the Spanish merchant ship fiasco. He walked down the line inspecting the prospective killicks and stopped dead in front of me. 'What are you doing here?' he demanded. 'We don't make up Skates!' (Skate I should explain is naval slang for naughty boy.)

I kept a poker face and he walked on and one by one the potential leading hands were ushered into the office by the Chief until at last it was my turn. He strode over to me and rasped, 'Attention!' then with a grin he said, 'Go on in. Left! Right! Left! Right!' and two minutes later I was a leading hand.

Gus and Dan

Meanwhile the war was drawing to a close. The Germans were taking a fearful pounding from both the East and the West as everyone tried to reach Berlin before their trusted allies. The air waves were full of confused U-boats who were running short of fuel, food and ammunition and had no base to return to as more and more ports were occupied by the Allies.

They were exciting times and the watches simply flew by as we got bearing after bearing on the desperate German subs, but inevitably it was Gus that stole the limelight. He was listening to Dan, a U-boat control station that had a silent period of five minutes after every fifteen minutes transmission and, of course, in the other ear he had Tokyo Rose who was still going strong from Japan urging our troops to abandon their lost cause — don't they have newspapers out there?

During Dan's silent periods which were very rarely used, something began signalling, but the something wasn't using the U-boats codes.

The Jackpot

Gus awoke with a start from his sexual reverie with the seductive Nip and thinking he must be off frequency tried to find it using his Tokyo Rose set. This promptly oscilated on other frequencies and alerted the control operator who demanded to know what Gus was up to.

'There's something funny going on with Dan', said Gus, desperately, so control plugged in to him and without more ado alerted Ascension Island and Tristan da Cuna to get a bearing on the mystery signal.

Gus hit the jackpot! A large German naval vessel was trying to get to South America and was frantically trying the U-boat frequencies as the usual channels were chaotic, to see if they had any better ideas. She was easily intercepted by our fleet in the South Atlantic and our skipper was congratulated by the powers that be and even Gus got a pat on the back, although he hadn't a clue what it was all about.

Something Amiss

The next day I met Molly at the Cotton Tree as per usual and although she smiled and gave me the warmest of kisses, I thought she seemed a trifle subdued and by the time we were aboard the loveboat I was sure something was amiss.

'Something troubling you, Molly?' I asked.

'Make love to me, David', she cried and pulled me fiercely towards her.

She gave herself to me with savage abandon and by the time we had finished, tears were streaming down her cheeks.

'Molly, darling, what on earth is the matter?' I whispered, tenderly holding her naked body close to mine.

'We're finished, David,' she sobbed and for ten minutes she poured her heart out to me trying to explain the complicated mess and the human emotions that meant we were to part for ever.

The Problem

I always knew that she had not told me the whole story but I was so happy with the way things were that I hadn't dared to ask. Now I knew the whole truth and was thankful that I hadn't known from the start or those wonderful halcyon days might never have been.

She was married, of course. A whirlwind romance

with an American flier (East Anglia was full of them in 1943) and a quick trip to the registry office and just as the wonder of it all had begun to wear thin, his Flying Fortress had been shot down over Germany with apparently no survivors. It was after six months with no news that Molly had decided to make the break and come out to Africa where we both met the love of our young lives.

So what's the problem?

The problem is that the advancing Allied Forces had captured a Germany military hospital and there lying in traction was Molly's husband, still alive but a mere shadow of the arrogant young airman of 1943.

He had arrived back in East Anglia two weeks ago and had written an impassioned letter to her begging her to come back to the States with him and nurse him back to health. He had thought of nothing but the moment when they would be together again, through all those months of agony in Germany and he knew that once she was with him again, he could make it.

Molly sobbed, 'I have to go to him, David. I'm a nurse and I am still his wife. I can't walk out on him now!'

'But Molly, I love you', I pleaded, 'and I know you love me, it can't just end like this'.

'Of course I love you, darling', she said, 'and I always will, but I can never see you again, you know that, don't you?'

I nodded dumbly and pressed her gorgeous body close to mine for the last time.

The Assyrian

We had barely finished dressing when I felt the boat drifting to the bank and as it touched, a large fat Assyrian gent climbed aboard and with the natural indignation of the owner, demanded to know what we were doing aboard his boat.

I could have explained in detail, but I don't think that was what he wanted, so instead I ushered Molly past him and helped her to disembark. I was just about to follow when he gave me a mighty thump in the back to help me on my way.

If it had been one of our normal love sessions I might have ignored it just to keep the peace, but today my emotions were full to bursting point and I was ready to explode. As soon as I whipped round and he saw the savage fury in my face, he knew he had pushed his luck too far. I swung my fist towards him, accelerated by a million pent-up emotions and it landed on his chest like a sledgehammer. He shot backwards over the rail and into four feet of oily, grey water and emerged spluttering to stand chest high with just the shoulders of his one hundred guinea suit above the water.

He watched boggle-eyed as I brandished my fist at him but made no attempt to come out of the water until we were well down the towpath.

At the Cotton Tree the Bedford was waiting and she kissed me passionately for the last time and went aboard. The most beautiful thing in my life had gone — for ever. I never saw Molly again, for she was granted compassionate leave and caught the next boat home. Fortunately I never saw the Assyrian again, either.

The Berlin Bunker

For a while I was like a bear with a sore head as I brooded on a Mollyless future and I was probably the second most self-pitying man in the war.

The first was ranting and raving in a Berlin bunker, surrounded by the last of the faithful and bemoaning the fact that his generals had let him down. By this time he was a nervous wreck, high on drugs and probably impotent in spite of the amorous attentions of Eva Braun who was to become Mrs Hitler for a few brief hours before the lunatic destroyed them both in a suicide pact.

The wedding ceremony was slightly delayed by some thirty minutes or so as Hitler was busy ordering the execution of one Herman Fegelein who had returned from the Eastern Front to become S.S. Leader Himmler's liaison officer with Hitler.

Desertion

Unfortunately in the final days of the war Himmler had abandoned his Fuhrer and was planning to negotiate a truce with the Allies, although he had more chance of opening up an ice cream parlour in Hell. By the time Hitler realised this it was too late to do anything about it for the Russians had already cut the road between Berlin and Himmler's headquarters at Hohenlychen.

However, General Fengelein had flown back to Berlin in a Junkers 52 but instead of reporting to the Fuhrer's bunker, he went straight to his mistress's flat where he spent an enjoyable two days in spite of the war that was tearing the city apart, before he was missed and an escort picked its way through the fighting to fetch him back to the bunker where he was tried for desertion and executed on Hitler's orders.

'Why do I introduce the General execution into Hitler's wedding?' you may well ask. I mention it simply because Herman Fegelein was married to a Fraulein named Gretl Braun and was Eva's brother-in-law and it did seem a trifle callous even by the Fuhrer's standards to hand him over to the Gestapo for a particularly painful death just an hour before he took Eva for his wife.

The End of Goebels

Although the buxom blonde knew of Fegelein's fate the only tears in her eyes at the wedding were tears of happiness. Even death was a small price to pay to marry her beloved Fuhrer.

The news of Hitler's and Eva's suicide pact spread swiftly through the bunker and not to be outdone, Dr Goebels promptly followed suit with his entire family, but at this moment in time there was still a fortnight or so to go before these earth shattering events took place, and for the moment the Doctor was still pouring forth his propaganda while the Fuhrer was issuing impossible orders to his beleaguered and often non-existant troops and the S.S. had a field day shooting down those that had retreated, often in the face of impossible odds.

A Miracle

All my immediate circle of friends were now killicks so I was pretty relieved not to be the odd one out and as Benny pointed out, we had now risen to the same rank as the 'little corporal' did in world war one. I just hoped we didn't finish up the same way that he appeared to be going in world war two.

At long last the miracle happened and the powers that be decided that West Africa could hold the fort without us. We had served more than three times the RAF tour of duty and nearly a year more than the navy's alloted span.

We were going home at last!

A lorry took us to a transit camp called Hastings and we felt every bit as good as William the Conqueror must have felt in 1066 at a similarly named venue as we hung around for a ship to take us back to dear old 'Blighty'.

It should have been pretty boring but on the contrary, there was a constant stream of incidents which made every day a talking point. I can't put them in chronological order, but I can certainly recall some of the highlights.

Green Mamba

There was an RAF chap in another hut who got under his mosquito net to find a green mamba had beaten him to it. The snake promptly bit him before it slithered out of the hut and the seriously ill airman was rushed to the General Hospital, which was cruel luck when you are on the last stage of your journey home.

At that time I didn't know that Molly was already on her way home so I brooded over the fact that he might well be nursed by my beloved angel just as I was beginning to forget her.

At the back of the camp was a ravine, on the other side of which was a native village with a couple of dingy bars. It was quite a long detour to reach the place but there was a large iron pipe that ran across the ravine and the daring or foolhardy or even desperately thirsty would crawl along the pipe to the unsavoury delights of the village.

Into the Ravine

The danger was not so much going across when you were sober, but traversing it coming back in the dark when you had had a skinful.

Inevitably we had a casualty. A lad from our hut lost

his grip and plunged into the ravine on his way back from the village, and he was in pretty bad shape when they rushed him off to 'Mollyland'.

The following night two natives got into our hut after lights out and rifled the ravine victim's locker which unfortunately was not locked. They were just leaving when one of the lads heard them and made a grab for the backmarker. The intruder dropped his haul but he was naked as a jaybird and covered in grease and our chap couldn't hold him. The marauders escaped across the pipeline and disappeared into the village.

The Victim's mates were so incensed at the outrage which seemed so much worse because they had stolen the lad's belongings while he was lying at death's door — although I doubt very much whether the thieves were aware of this.

The Raiding Party

However came the dawn and half a dozen of them formed a raiding party and went into the village and burned down a couple of huts as a reprisal. Surprisingly there was no protest from the villagers and no come-back or enquiry as to who had done it. I wondered if against all the odds they had actually burned down the right two huts and the Chief had the good sense to say 'it serves you right!'

The next highlight was a visit from 'Alice, Queen of Kissi'.

'She' was a sick berth attendant who had volunteered for an extra tour of duty in West Africa 'because there's a terrible shortage of women in Sierra Leone and the lads need me'.

She arrived in the mess one evening with her little entourage and certainly created a stir. With very little persuasion she stood on a table and began to sing and the effect was electrifying.

'Ave Maria'

Usually 'gays' make me want to puke, but for sheer talent this one was pretty special. She sang in a falsetto voice and you could hear a pin drop as that motley throng listened, completely enthralled. The climax of her act was a rendering of 'Ave Maria' and it was beautiful. To this day I can't hear that song without remembering 'Alice' and the absolute hush she instilled in the ultimate of demanding audiences.

During our second week at the transit camp, Germany surrendered and the war in Europe was over, which was a little frustrating for us safely tucked away in West Africa because it meant that we wouldn't be home for the VE night celebrations.

On the other hand if you happened to be a German soldier, short of food and ammunition and facing the Russian hordes all with murder in their hearts, I should think that the end of the war could not come quickly enough.

Free French

However we managed to celebrate in our own inimitable way. Everyone was drinking up and toasting Churchill, Monty and even Stalin when at the height of the festivities a Free French matelot began urinating on the floor in the centre of the canteen. An army corporal called him a dirty bastard and the resultant punch-up would have done credit to a Wild West movie.

The canteen was wrecked and we were lucky that our

draft chits weren't cancelled, but there were so many of us involved that it was easier just to get rid of us on the next boat.

The 'boat' in question proved to be the Mauritania which we boarded without any yellow arm bands and we had a marvellous and happy cruise back to Liverpool in a U-boat free ocean.

Two days out from England I sent a telegram to my parents saying, 'Won't be long now' and there we were back at the Liver Buildings.

The Queue

The customs men came aboard and went to the Ward Room for 'drinkies' and then set up tables on deck. You had to get a clearance chitty from them before you could go ashore and the word soon got around that the one on number three table was 'Brahms and Liszt', out of his mind with the result that an enormous queue formed at his desk while the others had a mere handful to deal with. fortunately I was in the first quarter of the favoured queue before they started doing anything about it and started sending the back half to the other tables.

I dragged my kitbag up to the beaming, bumbling drunk and was waved through with my precious chitty and felt as though I'd won the pools.

Soon we were going through the joining routine back at Chatham only now we could sleep in the barracks and not down the dreaded tunnel, and the following day I was going 'up to the smoke' on a month's foreign service leave, and was I ready for that! I'd got a lotta living to do!

Put the Flags Out

My mother was actually waiting at the gate when I arrived. With that sixth sense that mothers have, she walked down the path at exactly the moment I turned the corner of our street, yet she had no indication of even the day my leave started.

I realised with a start that my sister had put the flags out in readiness for the hero's return and once again, I was painfully aware that the real heroes were the ordinary working class people who had kept London and many other cities alive in spite of the bombs, the land mines, the doodlebugs and the rockets. The proof was everywhere in the acres of devastation that had once been people's homes.

My mother was plumper than I remembered her, probably on account of her wartime diet, but she was still her usual placid self. My father came out and joined us and the three of us did an impromptu jig in the front garden.

Neighbours came round to join the welcoming party and my father opened a bottle of scotch and another of port which he had been saving for the occasion, and soon it was just as though I had never been away.

'Shortage of Fellas'

That evening my pal Vic came round to rehabilitate me. Vic had been an apprentice at the small arms factory at Enfield Lock when the war started and was quite rightly in a reserved occupation for without skilled workers like him, the troops would not have the ammunition to wage war against the hated Boche. He was rolling in money but as he said with a touch of irony, the girls would still rather be seen with a stony broke squaddie or matelot than a rich civvy.

Our intention was to go to a dance where we would probably meet some of the old gang, but just as we were approaching the entrance two very attractive girls came up to us and said that they were having a party and there was a shortage of 'fellas' and would we come back with them and make the numbers up.

Talk about an offer you can't refuse!

We arrived just as they were struggling to get next door's piano into the front room and in no time at all I had taken the front door off its hinges and then the parlour door and with a protesting jangle of notes, the piano was in and the party was in full swing. It was a typical rowdy London knees-up with plenty of kissing and cuddling thrown in. The doors were still off when we left at four in the morning. Well, nobody burgled working class houses in those days, and tomorrow next door would want their piano back.

'Paradise Regained'

For the rest of that month's leave I did the rounds with Vic and met quite a few of the girls from my youth club days. They were now very much grown up young ladies and several had married and settled down and two were already widows.

I dated eighteen different girls on that leave, for with my uniform and Vic's money, plus the manpower shortage, we'd never had it so good. After the despair of West Africa I knew what Milton meant by 'Paradise Regained'. It was hard to believe that there were so many lovely girls available after Sierra Leone's ration of ten per thousand men.

There were moments of sadness too when I discovered the gaps in the ranks of my friends. Some were squaddies or matelots, but most of my closest friends had been air crew and there were four or five that I would never see again and a couple that were missing, but on the credit side two that we knew were in POW camps after baling out eventually came back to the fold. By the end of my leave I still had no steady girl friend and I knew I had not completely recovered from Molly, although I was having a satisfactory convalescence.

The Story Tellers

Back at Chatham we swapped leave stories. Toddy had found a widow in Wimbledon and Benny had blotted his copy book when seated at the Sunday lunch table. An uncle strode into the room and gave him a welcoming slap on the back and Benny who was still suffering pretty badly from prickly heat, screamed at the top of his voice, 'F***ing arseholes!' to an open mouthed family gathering.

Bugsie had returned to deepest Norfolk where apparently there were considerable pickings to be had amongst the Women's Land Army, but we weren't quite sure who picked who.

Gus's Party

Gus had managed to turn his Foreign Service leave into a disaster from the word go. He invited half a dozen of his friends back to his house in Brighton for a celebration party and half a dozen Brighton Belles had eagerly volunteered to balance the numbers.

The party started in a fairly orderly fashion with most of the guests smooching to the radiogram churning out

Bing Crosby's 'Moonlight Becomes You' and 'Moonlight Cocktails', but the medicine was far too potent for the patients and within half an hour, Gus was painfully aware that the only people left in the front room were himself and his partner.

In his own words, 'I went upstairs and there they were — all of them at it! On the landing, in the bedrooms and the bathroom. I threw them all out, every one of them. They turned my house into a brothel!'

Pompey

It came as quite a shock to us to realise that the war was not yet over and that there was still a considerable shemozzle going on in the Far East.

As a sharp reminder we were promptly drafted to Portsmouth for a crash course in Japanese morse and my heroic instincts flickered once again. We were fresh out of Germans, but it would be nice to have a crack at the Japs.

We had our usual runs ashore in between our studies. The Guildhall had two stone lions outside it, and Toddy informed us that every time a virgin walked past, they roared. Fred, who was inclined to be somewhat naive, actually stood and watched them.

The Magician

Bugsie found out that at the local variety theatre there was a magician who produced pints of beer out of nowhere and called for volunteers out of the audience to help him by drinking the stuff!

We agreed that a front row seat sounded like a good investment so Bugsie, Benny, Toddy and myself arrived early and secured the pole position for the evening show.

I can't remember much about the other acts but I can clearly remember the magician. Never had he procured his four volunteers so quickly. The challenge was barely out of his mouth than there were his four likely lads lined up on the stage. What Bugsie hadn't heard was that the magician also gave his volunteers a hard time. You get nothing for nothing in this world.

We were the butts of all his corny jokes and antics and were supposed not to notice when he removed your wallet or belt, even when he slipped it round your ankles.

A Foaming Pint

Eventually he produced four pints of beer from an apparently empty cask and that was the first time I was impressed. He lined us up and said the first one to empty his glass on the word 'go' would get another pint and added 'my money is on, Dave'.

I didn't let him down, after all I had been waiting two hours for that pint and I won in a common canter as they say. He cleared the stage except for myself and produced yet another foaming pint with a two inch head on it, but every time I tried to sink it he produced a feather duster and touched me up with it. He was thoroughly enjoying himself, so I raised the glass to my lips and blew with all my might and the froth went all over his face.

The audience loved it and I really thought he would be pleased that we'd brought the house down. Not a bit — he was furious. 'You bastard', he hissed, his face contorted with rage and then realising that the audience were expecting a better reaction, he mopped his face as

I finished my beer and with a fixed grin, ushered me off the stage.

Z Bar Hand Niglee

We perservered with our Japanese morse which proved ten times more difficult than German or Italian. They didn't even write across the page like any civilised nation and their letters were a nonsense to an English operator. To this day I can vaguely remember one symbol (yes, only one) which was a Z Bar Hand Niglee and went something like Da da dit dit da da dit dit da da dit dit. All that for just one letter, although I suspect that any Japanese operator will correct me. Well, it was nearly fifty years ago.

Z Bar Hand Niglee or not, we completed the course and by the beginning of August 1945 we were issued with a draft chit to Trincomalee which was the naval base in Ceylon, which they now tell me is called Sri Lanka (don't ask me why). I was really keen on this one, no water rationing, no maleria and a climate where white women could thrive. I.E. Wrens galore.

Enola Gay

Unfortunately no-one had told us about 'Manhatten Project' and 'Enola Gay', who between them managed to drop an atom bomb on Hiroshima just as we were waiting for our boat to dreamland. It was followed quickly by a second atom bomb on Nagasaki and the Japs had no alternative but to surrender and all bets to Trincomalee were off.

Highlights

VJ Day seemed almost anti-climax when it arrived. After six years of earnest endeavour my war effort was hardly the stuff that heroes were made of. I looked back at the highlights of my distinguished career.

Firewatches galore, but not one rescue (unless you count the old lady in the lavatory). Air crew training but no plane. Naval training but no ship. A bayonet jabbed in the rear of what was probably one of our own workmen. A close encounter with the enemy when we pushed the Wop POWs off the pavement and boarding a neutral merchantman in harbour to 'capture' it.

There was, of course, the punch-up with the Free French on VE night, but as we were supposed to be on the same side, I wouldn't get many merit marks for that little episode. Then there was the tapping of heads while patrolling the detention centre and, of course, the tapping of Gabby's head which gave me almost as much pleasure as a medal.

Finally, there was the fat Assyrian that I had thumped for pushing me off his boat, which reminded me vividly of Molly. I was surprised to realise that it no longer pained me to think of her — just a warm glow that would remain a fond memory for ever.

Celebrations

Meanwhile the country was about to celebrate a famous victory and although we were the duty watch we had no specific task to pin us down, so Toddy and I quietly slipped away into Cosham for refreshment. Everyone was hugging and kissing everyoine else so it didn't take too much organising for two sex-starved matelots to find two very pretty Wrens and start hugging and kissing them — purely to demonstrate our feelings of national pride of course.

A few drinks later and I suggested that the obvious place to celebrate VJ Day was at Southsea where HMS Victory was reclining, although I understand her skipper was no longer aboard. So we unanimously agreed that Southsea was the 'in place' and the four of us boarded the bus to Britain's best known ship of the line.

The Jap

A small crowd had already gathered and were singing and dancing and I was surprised to see a sinister-looking oriental leaping up and down and making Kung Fu gestures at everybody. I could well imagine him giving our lads a hard time as they built the bridge over the River Kwai, and I asked the obvious question, 'What's a Jap doing celebrating VJ Day?'

My Wren giggled as she explained 'He owns the Chinese restaurant in town'.

We spent a couple of happy hours drinking and dancing before we eventually bade the Victory a sailor's farewell and strolled arm in arm to the beach.

Make Love Not War

There was an hour left to sunset and as the sun sank lower in the direction of the Isle of Wight, Eileen, my Wren, snuggled up to me in the time-honoured fashion. I drew her closer and gave her a passionate kiss that had nothing to do with VJ Day and we celebrated the end of the war by making love.

We were back at Chatham with two schools of thought. Those who had wives or regular girl friends at home were over the moon at not being shipped off to the Far East, and the rest of us who had joined the navy to see the world (God help it!) were pretty despondent.

At Chatham we were dispersed to outlying camps at Hoo, Cookham and Laughing Water (or 'Chuckling Piss' as it was affectionately called). Here my antics on the 'Ware' caught up with me again, and while all the rest of the Special Operators were sent to Cookham, I finished up at Hoo with all the orthodox telegraphists.

The Route March

Once again my limitations as a straight telegraphist were exposed, only more so for I was now a one badge killick and should have known the job backwards, but it didn't matter twopence any more for it was their mistake this time and, in any case, I was in no position to endanger a whole convoy.

The Chief just told me to look busy round the camp until they sorted it out and to fall in for the route march at 10 a.m. each morning. I was not terribly keen on the idea of a route march, but to my amazement everyone in the hut fell over themselves to get on parade and insisted that I did the same.

With some reluctance I 'fell in three deep' and marched out of the gate with my new shipmates, all of whom strode out eagerly to the village. At the beginning of the High Street, the Chief called us to a halt and would you believe it, we were bang outside the village inn.

'Parade will remuster in one hour. Parade dis—miss!'

I had palled up with a couple of Geordies and we found that we could just comfortably drink three pints in the hour, which was a round apiece. The bad news was that between the village inn and nipping up to London at the weekends was putting a severe strain on my budget which I partly solved by dipping into the ticket collector's box at six a.m. one morning when he was presumably answering a call of nature, and from then on I had an assortment of tickets all the way to Rochester, Chatham and Gillingham.

Tickets Galore

Among my collection of tickets were two Dartford to Chatham returns, so rather than waste them, I suggested to one of my Geordie pals that we visited the seamen's mission and stayed overnight in Dartford, returning the following morning. The third member of our drinking party had been roped in for guard duty that evening, so he readily agreed.

We duly arrived in Dartford that afternoon and spent a pleasant couple of hours or so sightseeing, which included not only the historical buildings, but every pretty girl above the age of seventeen. As Geordie One remarked, 'there's nothing like being away from women for a year or two to make you incredibly randy' — it was a statement I could not refute.

By seven o'clock we were installed in a pub that had been recommended by one of the 'barrach stanchions' and relaxed over a couple of foaming pints. There was not as much talent as our informant had forecast but at a table across the room were two very attractive girls.

The bad news was that they were accompanied by two stokers, but the good news was that both matelots were dead drunk even at that early stage of the evening. We gave them another half an hour until one was nearly asleep and the other had staggered to the heads and barely made it back to the table, and decided the time was ripe to move in and make them a better offer.

The girls readily agreed to desert the sinking ship and

moved across to our table while the stokers blinked blearily at Geordie who stood well over six feet tall and decided that they were in no condition to do anything about it. The pairing off was easily resolved as Pearl was a couple of inches taller than I was and went straight to Geordie's side of the table, while Helen was petite and around five feet four and slipped easily and naturally beside me on the bench seat.

The next couple of hours simply flashed by as we drank up, swapped stories and indulged in kissing and cuddling, and by closing time I was thoroughly aroused by this pretty little Maid of Kent who kissed so passionately and persistently found my tongue with hers. As we left the pub arm in arm, we all knew what the score was and when I asked Helen if she knew of a quiet spot, she nodded to an empty barn across the way.

Once inside Geordie took his Pearl behind some convenient bales of straw and Helen and I found a similar venue at the other end. I spread my Burbery on the straw, for there has been many a love match ruined by trying to become passionate while the lady is being pierced by the stalks, and we snuggled down on my raincoat.

At last I was becoming competent at removing ladies' undergarments in a seductive manner rather than ripping them off in desperation, and I was relieved to discover that she was wearing French knickers which was the ultimate turn-on in the forties, for she was so enthusiastic that I would not have been surprised if she had worn none at all. To the matelot's mind the distinction between wearing knickers or not was the difference between a pro and an enthusiastic amateur, and I'd always hated the idea of paying for it as completely destroying the beauty of the sex act.

None of these thoughts, however, did I pass on to the lovely Helen whose face was indeed pretty enough to launch a thousand ships, albeit from Chatham, and soon we were locked together in a frenzy of desire, her delighted moans echoed round the barn and neither of us could care less. We lay there fondling each other after our climax and she was so desirable that I managed to arouse myself once more, which pleased her immensely for she still had so much love to give.

Eventually Geordie's booming voice called all hands to muster outside the barn and we walked the girls home, and parted with promises to return as soon as we could. In the event I never did as I was drafted out of Hoo two days later, but I'll wager Geordie One took Geordie Two back there as soon as I'd gone.

We strolled back to the seamen's mission and soon I was tucked up in my bunk and in the land of nod, dreaming of the beautiful Helen and how we would make music together as soon as I could get back to Dartford.

I was awakened by the door of the dormitory crashing open and a drunken matelot staggering in, singing and shouting at the top of his voice.

'All right, pipe down!' I bellowed in my best Leading Hand's voice.

Still the noise continued unabated as the drunk leaned on the bottom end of my bunk (I was on the top tier) and sang the praises of Maggie May.

Furiously, I shouted, 'Shut up, or I'll shut you up!' and sat up in my bunk. Just as I propped myself up on my elbows the drunk lurched round to the side of my bed and lunged forward, hitting me straight in the eye with a left hook, which knocked me flat on my back again, then he turned and scarpered through the door laughing like a maniac.

I leapt out of bed wearing only my pants and vest which is the matelot's traditional sleeping apparel in home waters, and rushed to the door but it was too late.

I could hear him jogging down the street, still making his lunatic noises and I abandoned the chase and returned to my bunk, but this time my dreams of Helen were shattered and only the drunk came up on the screen.

Next morning I compared notes with Geordie and we both agreed that he looked remarkably similar to the stoker whose girls we had pinched in the pub, although he'll never have the satisfaction of knowing he hit the right bloke.

By the time we got back to camp I had developed a 'right shiner' and by the time Geordie had explained it to all my mates they had the impression that I'd seduced this stoker's girl, so he thumped me, which wasn't quite how I saw it, but to lie on the straw with Helen while she fiercely gave me her young and beautiful body, I would cheerfully go through it all again.

I was somewhat relieved when they eventually sorted me out and returned me to my regular pals who were sharing Cookham Camp with the Borstal Boys. I could not have kept the pace at Hoo up for much longer for in the evenings we were now returning to the inn for another three pints and the novelty was wearing thin.

The Perfidious Albion

On 5th July 1945 Churchill confidently held a general election, knowing that he was the idol of the country, the hero of the hour.

What he hadn't allowed for was the 'Perfidious Albion' for thousands of troops (myself included) thought that Winnie was a fantastic leader against Hitler, but once the war was over he and the class they represented would treat the working class like serfs once again. So to the utter amazement of the rest of the world (not to mention the Tories) the Labour Party led by Clement Atlee romped home by 393 to 213. And another hero bit the dust!

The Borstal Boys

Life at Cookham was much more energetic and we played soccer against the Borstal Boys, many of whom I found were in there deliberately in order to beat the call-up.

We soon learned not to leave our gear on the touch-lines for they were soon crowded with Borstal lads and the chances of anything being there at the end of the match was pretty remote.

Cockles was now back in Blighty sporting his wings (he had been even less involved in the war than I had, but that uniform sure attracted the girls) and he lost no time in arranging a get-together.

I had a weekend pass ('Friday while' in naval parlance) and got a travel warrent to Blackpool where he was entrenched with his air crew buddies and we had a fabulous session of wine, women and song — what I can remember of it, although I vaguely remember Reginald Dixon playing his heart out at the Tower Ballroom.

We parted in the small hours at Blackpool station, accompanied by a couple of girls whose names escape me and agreed that next time Cockles would come south.

Southend Pier

Three weeks later I received a letter from him saying he would be on Southend Pier at 1700 hours on Saturday and he was confident I'd be there. It was quite a tricky journey from Cookham to Southend but I made it in good time and waited just inside the entrance.

By 1720 there was still no sign of him and I began to get fidgety. Which end of the pier did he mean? Southend Pier is the longest in the country and a train took you the one and a quarter miles to the end if you didn't fancy the walk.

By 1730 I took the plunge and boarded the train and five minutes later I am reconnoitring the end of the pier in search of a missing pilot.

I Pass

Needless to say I drew a blank and boarded the train returning to the entrance.

Halfway there we passed the other train going to the end of the pier and in the instant we passed I saw Cockles waving his arms and shouting, although I couldn't make out a word of it, but at least we had found each other — or had we?

Back at the entrance I pondered over my next move. Would he wait at the end for me, or was he coming back? It was the sort of situation that could go on indefinitely. Ships that pass in the night took on a new meaning. I decided to sit tight and after a pregnant pause he alighted from the incoming train grinning with delight, quite unmoved by the fact that it was an hour and ten minutes later than advertised.

But the night was still young and as any Londoner will tell you, there's no finer place than Southend to let your hair down.

Anti-Climax

By 1946 Britain was innundated with troops returning from overseas and at long last demobilisation had started, yet amazingly the call-up system was still operating.

I could think of nothing more depressing than joining the army just as the war had finished. It was the pinacle of anti-climax.

However the lads I spoke to some years later reckoned that being part of the army of occupation in Germany was the highlight of their young lives, although there was no fraternization allowed — not much!

Mary

In January 1946 I met Mary who was to become the new love in my life, and at last I had a steady girl friend. My supply of tickets to London Bridge was by now exhausted but usually one of the gang had some to spare for you can only use a limited number of three day returns yourself — the monthly returns were like gold dust.

So I was now going 'up to the smoke' three times a week and life was looking good. Mary and I would go round the funfairs or skating or dancing with our friends at The Royal, Tottenham, or a stroll round Pymmes Park and a boat on the lake. They were halcyon days with the war a million miles behind us.

Never a Hero

They were getting rid of the navy in double quick time and by March I was poised to return to civvy street. In the event there was the inevitable hiccup and I finally walked out of Chatham Barracks in my brand new demob suit in May 1946 with over £60 in my pocket. Wow!

I wasn't a hero, but Mary didn't care — her man was home all in one piece and that was quite sufficient for her. Surprisingly, I didn't care either. It had been an experience that I would never have had in a printshop and here I was, nearly twenty-three years of age and fit as a fiddle in spite of all my kamikaze efforts.

I think a fitting sub-title for my book should be, 'Or if you're lucky, they won't let you get yourself killed'.